How to
Talk to Me
After I'm Gone

About the Author

Alexandra Chauran is a second-generation fortuneteller and a professional psychic intuitive. For more than a decade, she has served thousands of clients in the Seattle area and globally through her website. She is certified in tarot and has been interviewed on National Public Radio and other major media outlets. Alexandra is currently pursuing a doctoral degree, lives in Issaquah, Washington, and can be found online at EarthShod.com.

To Write the Author

If you wish to contact the author or would like more information about this book, please write to the author in care of Llewellyn Worldwide, and we will forward your request. Both the author and publisher appreciate hearing from you and learning of your enjoyment of this book and how it has helped you. Llewellyn Worldwide cannot guarantee that every letter written to the author can be answered, but all will be forwarded. Please write to:

Alexandra Chauran
℅ Llewellyn Worldwide
2143 Wooddale Drive
Woodbury, MN 55125-2989

Please enclose a self-addressed stamped envelope for reply, or $1.00 to cover costs. If outside the USA, enclose an international postal reply coupon.

HOW TO
TALK TO ME
AFTER I'M GONE

Creating a Plan
for Spirit Communication

ALEXANDRA CHAURAN

Llewellyn Publications
Woodbury, Minnesota

FIRST EDITION
First Printing, 2014

Book design by Bob Gaul
Cover design by Lisa Novak
Cover art: iStockphoto.com/19912569/©subjug 40
         iStockphoto.com/11910847/©Barcin 20
         iStockphoto.com/7240600/©wragg 40
         iStockphoto.com/9328998/©Cecilia Bajic 15
         iStockphoto.com/5943477/©winterling 3
         iStockphoto.com/491733/©GildedCage 25
         Shutterstock/87997603/©Tsyhun
         Shutterstock/119239909/©Natalia Siverina
         Dreamstime/29906762/©Mazor
Cover photo: Alexandra Chauran
Editing by Laura Graves

Llewellyn Publications is a registered trademark of Llewellyn Worldwide Ltd.

Library of Congress Cataloging-in-Publication Data
Chauran, Alexandra, 1981–
  How to talk to me after I'm gone: creating a plan for spirit
communication/Alexandra Chauran.—First Edition.
      pages cm
  Includes bibliographical references.
  ISBN 978-0-7387-3925-0
1. Spiritualism. I. Title.
  BF1261.2.C475 2014
  133.9—dc23
                                   2014029581

Llewellyn Publications
A Division of Llewellyn Worldwide Ltd.
2143 Wooddale Drive
Woodbury, MN 55125-2989
www.llewellyn.com

Printed in the United States of America

Dedication

This book is dedicated to my children, Eris and Orion, my nieces, Angelina, Meira, Shiloh, and Dorothy, and to all my descendants yet to be born. It is also personally dedicated to you, the reader, and to anyone else who may talk to me and others like me after we die.

Acknowledgments

In writing this book, I first want to thank my gods: the Lady of life in whose arms I rest in certainty and the Lord of death and resurrection, for inspiring me to write this book through a vision in a dream. I'd also like to thank my ancestors, on whose shoulders I stand, without whom I would not be.

I am thankful always for my mother, Jean Pawlucki, for being the second set of eyes to see this book and for her tireless proofreading efforts. I'm grateful for my acquisitions editor, Amy Glaser, for the boundless energy she uses to support, guide, and enthuse any whose lives she touches. I'm thankful for my production editor Laura Graves for generosity with her time and attention and for making revisions and edits as painless a process as humanly possible. I'd also like to express gratitude for the visionaries in the Llewellyn art department for their cover art wizardry, and the marketing and publicity folks for all the magic they do.

Finally, I'd like to thank my husband and children for putting up with the mother of this household while she struggles with a serious addiction to writing books.

Contents

Introduction

They say that life is terminal. And that's what suddenly occurred to me when my doctor gave me the bad news: I had just been diagnosed with polycystic kidney disease, an eventually fatal illness, and I was still in my twenties. The reality of death came into sharp focus for the first time, much like the many tiny dark cysts that had shown up on the ultrasound of my kidneys. They were visual proof of the sense of mortality I would always carry with me. And these days, I am constantly aware that my body will never function any better than it does today.

"Now you know why I couldn't tell you the results of your tests over the phone," my doctor said. He was laughing and didn't seem to acknowledge my horror. Yes, I knew this condition could be hereditary, but the plan had been to donate one of my kidneys to mom so I could grant her many more years of healthy life. After all, cancer had taken my father from me only three years prior. My mother's kidneys were failing, and now I was learning that my own kidneys were destined to follow. We suffered from the same genetic death sentence.

Fast forward a few months and I was pregnant, praying for my mom while she underwent surgery that I'll experience one day myself, if I get the chance. I felt the same sense of dread my own children will probably have. At the same time, though, I now recognize that I am lucky—I know what will most likely kill me. When my mom was my age, she didn't have the knowledge that would inform the way she'd live her life. And I suspect that most of you reading this book don't have this kind of information, though we might each have a potential time bomb ticking away within our body.

Do you consider yourself a spiritual or faithful person? If not, I'd like to pass that certainty of the continuation of life after death to you. I believe that the spirits of deceased ancestors and even complete strangers can communicate with me. But, what good is a belief in spirit communication if nobody talks to me after I am dead and gone? This book is a spirit lifeline for the faithful like me, or for those who are merely open minded and hope to never be forgotten.

Starting with instructions on how to incorporate the conceptual cycles of death and rebirth into your everyday life, we'll separate the fear of the unknown from the reality of death by acknowledging it as a fact of life. These exercises have arisen spontaneously in many cultures at once, proving that they are essential to the human experience of life beyond the grave. You'll learn simple practices that will create bonds with friends and family that can last an eternity, and how to let go of any dusty old coping mechanisms that no longer serve you.

Next is the fun part—a crash course in learning spirit communication. This practice can be passed along to any loved ones you'll want to keep in touch with after you're gone, giving all of you the much-needed practice to live your beliefs in the future. Moving on, you'll begin implementing a workbook of your hopes and dreams for a future beyond this lifetime. You'll learn how you can express yourself once you're a part of the beauty of the spirit world, as well as how to communicate your wishes to continue your relationships long after you've left your body behind. The process of developing a means to call up ancestral spirits is ancient. It has been passed nearly unchanged through families for generations, and in this book I can gift it to you and yours.

Finally, I'd like to help you to explore your own beliefs about what happens after death and who or what may be waiting for you. Informed by your growing faith, we'll transport your beliefs beyond the barrier of taboo. I want you to shine your light of hope onto your family, friends, and community. From the unknown, certainty and peace can emerge.

But enough talking the talk; I'd like to walk the walk, if you'd please join me. To show you how simple and life-affirming this process can be, I want you, the reader, to summon and talk to my spirit after I have died. I'll teach you how to talk to me after I'm gone and invite you to pass along the knowledge of this practice for your own everlasting benefit.

How to Use This Book

If you read nothing else, make sure to turn to chapter 2. Read the instructions and complete the workbook in chapter 4 that explores your wishes regarding spirit communication with your surviving family and others. You should write it out or type it on the computer and email it to loved ones. You could also print it out and put it in a fire safe or safety deposit box with your will and other important documents. You can even post your answers publicly on the Internet. It's possible to pencil your thoughts straight into this book, but it's ultimately easier if they are kept with other important documents.

If you'd like to read this book from start to finish, you'll have a step-by-step guide to the basic concepts of life after death, the exploration of spirit communication, and the application of these ideas to yourself and loved ones who have died. Working through the chapters in order will help you to experience confidence and even joy in the face of death. Keep this book and work through it again in a few years to see if your beliefs have shifted through life experience. You might have more notes to add.

If there are other people in your life you would like to see live on after death through spirit communication, give them a copy of this book; the workbook section does not lend itself well to quickly reading and returning to a friend—it is a reference book. You can appreciate the process more by reviewing and revising your thoughts, as this is a serious matter to ponder over time yet undertake with immediacy and mindfulness. As a teacher, priestess, and interfaith chaplain, I've helped many people avoid regrets at the end of their lives by helping them prepare for their new existence on the other side. I hope to help you and your loved ones through this book for generations.

CHAPTER ONE

Getting Started—Living Without Fear of Death

A year before my dad died, he was at my handfasting, celebrating my new marriage to my husband. He told me, "now I can die happy." Ten days before he died, he got the medical scare that let him know the end was near. His kidneys shut down, and he had a brief stay in the hospital. When I spoke with him on the telephone, I tried to joke with him to cheer him up and keep the situation light, worried that he was feeling the same fear I was about death, knowing that he was going to be released from the hospital soon to return home. We spoke about special days of the year we always remember together and, still woozy from the treatment, he confirmed wearily, "Yes, we'll always have that." His parting words were "I love you."

About a week later, he lapsed into a coma. I was a thousand miles away, attending college. A nurse let me call her cell phone so that she could put it by his ear. Tearfully, I told him that he didn't have to hold on any longer. I knew he would want to hang on to be there for my graduation, even if he was comatose in a wheelchair, but I told him that didn't have to happen. I explained that I knew he would be there in spirit. Witnesses said he smiled. He waited a few more days, just to make sure that family friends arrived to take care of his wife before he died.

You don't have to rid yourself entirely of the fear of death before successfully preparing to communicate after you are gone or even before communicating with spirits yourself. But you can lay the groundwork for making spirit communication part of your life and family. Confronting your own fear of death head on can help you to avoid the pitfall of procrastination when preparing your own plans or those of others. Transforming your view of death into one of positive understanding instead of avoidance can also make this process feel more fun and, dare I say it, even life-affirming.

Death is scary; let's get that out of the way right up front. Almost all of us have a natural and healthy fear of death that keeps us from walking out in front of a bus and helps us rally to fight when we come down with an illness. But some people fear death more than others, and the fear is more prominent for some people than others. Why is that? Let's begin by exploring some reasons for fearing death.

- Fear of pain. What if dying hurts?

- Fear of a loss of control. I can't stop death from coming for me, and once it starts happening I will not be in charge of the process.

- Fear of the unknown. What is death like? What is being dead like?

- Fear of losing the sum total of one's personality, memories, and life experiences. The lifelong masterpiece work of art that is you could be destroyed forever.

- Fear of leaving the relationships, duties, and tasks you currently have. What will my kids do if I die? What about all of the things I have left undone?

- Fear of the afterlife. What if there is a hell? What if there is a void with no spirit life at all?

Worse yet, fear can be compounded by guilt over feeling fearful. After all, one might feel foolish or selfish by having anxiety about a process that definitely will happen to everybody someday. Those who are faithful and believe in a pleasant afterlife might think that fear shows a lack of trust in the divine; after all, theoretically the afterlife should lead to bliss, right?

I'll let you in on one of our society's best kept secrets: death doesn't have to be scary, and in fact it often isn't.

Sure, on the news we hear about violent deaths. One of the deaths that is most likely to be witnessed is that of a horrible car accident. But I'd like to share with you just a few of the peaceful deaths I've witnessed as a hospital chaplain. I served in the busiest trauma hospital in the tri-state area, so a typical day included many lives ending. I would sit in the spiritual care office, walk rounds, work my way through a checklist of the special requests of patients or sleep in a cot in a dormitory building at night, waiting for a pager to go off. Oftentimes the contact on this pager would be a nurse who was preparing a family to take somebody off life support. Sometimes it would buzz with an emergency code, letting me know that somebody was leaving his or her life unexpectedly.

One Christmas Eve I was spending the night at the hospital. That's one way that, as a non-Christian, I could help the Christian chaplains so they could be at home with their families. I was paged during the early evening to visit a woman who was going to be taken off life support. She was the matriarch of a huge family, and she was clearly loved. She lay in a coma, her grey gossamer hair spread out around her fluffy pillows as if it had been lovingly brushed. A young woman was gently washing the elder's face, and a small child was reading her a story. The old woman looked peaceful, as if she was only sleeping.

I introduced myself and spoke with them a moment before the nurse began to explain the procedure. In a moment, some medicine would arrive to help make Grandma more comfortable, then the life support would be removed. After life support removal, there was no telling how long it would take her body to shut down. She might die in minutes, or it might take days. As the nurse left to prepare the medicine, I allowed family members to speak with me as they wished. Grandma's daughter told me that her mom had been hanging on leading up to the holidays. As the matriarch of the family, she had a strong sense of duty, and it was as if she didn't want to let her family down. Now, though, she was in a brain-dead coma, and her daughter confided to me that she felt the spirit had already mostly left the body and was just clinging ever so tenuously. It was the spirit, not the body, that watched now.

The nurse returned and administered medicine through intravenous drip, asking the family if they wanted to say any last goodbyes. They bid Grandma goodbye, but rather than looking at the face of her body, no longer a vehicle for the mind that they had known in life, they stared upwards somewhere towards the ceiling, where it could be imagined her spirit was floating in the room. A doctor arrived and answered a few last-minute questions before the pulsing machines keeping Grandma alive were shut off. When the doctor turned them off and silenced the alarms, the room was eerily quiet. The nurse gently removed the tubes and monitors from Grandma's face. Everyone in the room waited with baited breath. Grandma's body continued to take feeble, shallow breaths of its own. Her family prayed quietly.

After an hour, I had to leave to serve other patients, but I let the family know that I was only a pager call away. Throughout the night, I checked on Grandma's room. There was always a family member or two with her, never leaving her side. They would take turns using the bathroom or sleeping. Her daughter, however, never rested, determined to be at Grandma's side when her spirit glided out of the room, away from the body and off to other realms.

In the morning, the family was still there. A kindly gentleman let me know that he was worried about Grandma's daughter, since she hadn't eaten or slept. I watched as her family gently cajoled her, asking her to join them for breakfast. There were only five family members left in the hospital that morning, and she was scared to leave Grandma alone. She asked me if I would stay in the room. I promised that I would, and I began my solitary vigil. As soon as the elevator doors closed across the faces of her exhausted family, I watched Grandma's body heave a gentle sigh and felt the chill of the spirit sliding from the room with force. It was over. I sprinted down the hallway and punched the button to open the elevator doors, but it was too late.

After doctors confirmed the death, I headed down to the cafeteria to find the family and pull them aside for the news. They were devastated that Grandma had waited until they were out of the room to leave. I tried to comfort the daughter by explaining that I had seen that phenomenon happen many times before. The family all agreed that Grandma's personality was such that she would have wanted some degree of privacy. She simply would not want to die in front of her loved ones. The family didn't even want to see the body after the spirit had left the room. They headed home to get some rest and move forward with their grief and their holiday.

Another peaceful death I recall was one that actually started out tragically. I was paged to an area of the hospital that had been restricted, which typically happens when a patient is a criminal, has been involved in a violent crime, or has been transferred from a prison. When I arrived, police filled the hallway. I checked the patient's file and to my surprise, discovered that the situation was rather unusual. The patient had been involved in a gang shooting, and was mainly in a restricted area to prevent rival gang members from coming in to finish the job themselves.

Sadly, the eighteen-year-old patient was being taken off of life support. When I entered the room, the young boy was lying in bed, the spirit still clinging to the body. The room was filled with other young people, about a dozen of them crowding around the bed and even sitting on countertops and a windowsill. These "family" members were all wearing pained expressions of sadness, anger, and regret, but the patient's face was calm and unknowing as he slept in his permanent coma. As I waited and chatted with some of the family members, the medical staff prepared to turn off life support. I overheard the young gang members murmuring about what had happened and discussing the people who were present at the shooting. I became aware that the violence would probably be continued with a retaliation against the rival gang, and I wished that the police officers guarding the hallways were listening in.

Two of the older boys, who were still probably in their early twenties, were muttering the street names of guys they saw at the shooting. "I'm going to go back to his house and light it up," one boy said. His face was a dark mask of rage. I made eye contact with him and he looked away, mumbling "that was my brother." He waved dismissively at the limp patient in the bed. I looked over at the youthful face, partially covered with dressings that discreetly hid the gunshot wound in his head. A young woman was leaning over him. She was a beautiful girl with curly hair that fell gently to her shoulders. Her deep brown eyes were accented with small tattoos of tears, oddly appropriate for the moment. She held the patient's hand and spoke to him softly in lilting Spanish.

As a doctor administered the medication and began the shutdown process for the life support, the girlfriend of the patient leaned forward and pressed a sweet kiss onto his cheek. This time, the death process did not take a day. As soon as life support was removed, the boy's chest stopped moving, and we all watched as his body seemed to transform into something plastic and unreal as the spirit left him. I could see the shadow of his spirit out of the corner of my eye as I gazed at his girlfriend. She sat up with a start, her eyes shooting skyward, her lips moving in silent prayer.

"I can hear his voice, you guys," she said, with a thick accent. Tears ran down her young cheeks. She looked back down at the body, then at the group of people in the room listening intently to her. "He don't have pain no more. He don't have no worries. He wants us to have no worries, too, see? He wants the hate to stop with him." She looked at the man who had expressed vengeful feelings. "Don't you go pop nobody over this."

He dropped his eyes to the floor in response and mumbled back, "but it's what he would have wanted." The girl stood up and took his hand.

"Things are different for him, now. He's in heaven, dude, he got heavenly wants. He wants peace now for all of us, so we gotta carry that on." The boy wiped a tear from his face and leaned forward in a heavy hug. As they embraced, the room filled with the sniffles of young people shedding tears. I found my own eyes heavy with tears, too. Unfortunately, there was little time for anyone to pay respects to the body; it had to be transferred to a special morgue because of the criminal nature of the death. But the kids were allowed to stay in the room a while longer. Each said goodbye to the spirit they felt lingering there. Indeed, the memory of that spirit experience has stayed with me to this day.

The last story I want to share is one that represents a typical death in the hospital. An elderly woman with a cute name (we'll call her "Goldie") was also in a coma and being readied for life support to be removed. Her family did not come to join her at the time of her death as is quite common for those who don't feel they can handle the experience. When I came to her, she was surrounded by kindly nurses who seemed to have taken a liking to the old woman. Rumors fly among nurses, and there were stories I had heard that several of the nurses could hear Goldie's spirit talking to them, telling them stories about her long and colorful life.

As I watched Goldie's interminable sleep, I could tell she must have been a character; she had a quirk of a smile and deep laugh lines in her dark skin. The nurses had made what I thought was an odd request for a CD player from the Spiritual Care department, so I had it with me. One nurse took out a CD that she had brought from home that was labeled simply, "Lullabies." I raised my eyebrows at her.

"What," said the nurse, eyeing me defensively. "Goldie requested it and I want to honor her wishes." I nodded, and looked over at Goldie's bed, startled by what seemed to be movement out of the corner of my eye.

Now, I am more sensitive than most, so I wasn't exactly shocked when it appeared that I was seeing double. Goldie's spirit, to me, appeared just like the woman in the bed, only she was sitting upright next to her body, clothed in vibrant attire that contrasted with the pale blankets and hospital gown I saw when I came into the room. Spirit Goldie's hair was carefully styled, and I saw that she wore gold-rimmed glasses with colorful beads trailing to a necklace around her neck. When she laughed, she tilted her head back and placed one hand at her collarbone, obviously tickled by the nurse's defense of her lullaby choice. She fixed her brown eyes on me and said, "It's like childhood, honey. It's a comfort for me. It reminds me of being with Maw Maw and Paw Paw. Like I'm going to be soon."

I nodded and seated myself as the nurses busied themselves with the preparations. I knew they must have been able to see and hear Goldie in some way to honor her requests, but I still felt strange about talking to her while they were in the room, lest I seemed like I was having a conversation with thin air. I chanced it anyway. "My name is Alex, and I'm a chaplain. How can I help you?" Goldie's spirit smiled sweetly at me, as if I were a small child she was humoring. "Pray with me, sweetheart. The Lord's Prayer." I reached forward to grasp the hand of Goldie's still living body, a little nervous since I didn't really have the Lord's Prayer memorized. I didn't have to worry, though. As I gripped the warmth of Goldie's hand, her spirit's voice boomed loud and clear, as if Goldie were reciting it for an entire church congregation. "Our Father, who art in heaven…"

The nurses finished administering medicine and slowly removed the life support devices from Goldie's body. The room quieted, and for a moment, all we could hear was the lullaby music and Goldie's body drawing slow and shallow breaths. Goldie's spirit began to croon along with the instrumental lullaby that was playing, swaying back and forth and tilting her head as if in ecstasy from the music. The moment Goldie's body died was marked only by her spirit slipping easily off the bed and beginning to dance, shrugging shoulders with joy and turning around smoothly, unencumbered by earthly arthritis or old knees. And just like that, I couldn't see her spirit anymore. But I was sure that it was still dancing.

What is a Spirit?

For the purposes of this book, a spirit is defined as a non-corporeal entity with personality and motivations informed from a human's life. Spirits sometimes communicate with living humans by showing themselves, speaking aloud, or through the use of spirit communication tools and techniques. You might already be familiar with one type of spirit; an apparition. Often called a "ghost," an apparition is a spirit that can appear to be opaque, translucent, or transparent to be visible for the living. In many cultures, what happens next can elevate beloved ancestors to legendary status.

Consider, for example, the experience of Vodou practitioners in huts called peristyles across Haiti. Mambos (priestesses) and houngans (priests) gather with the community to honor God and ancestors who have achieved archetypical ranks of near sainthood or divinity by helping out their descendants and Vodouisants for generations. Vodou Priestess Marie Laveau even grants wishes beyond the grave in New Orleans to visitors who inscribe "XXX" on her tomb. More about the Vodou culture, saints, and how you can keep working on climbing the spiritual ranks even after you are dead will be included in chapter 3 on beliefs.

Why Try to Continue Communication After Death?

Let's imagine a middle-aged man named Leo. Leo's mom died when he was a young man, and yet he still maintains a relationship with her. When she was still alive and he was in college, he used to call her every week and talk to her on the phone. Spirit communication replaced that phone call but is still an important part of his week. Leo's mom always respected his beliefs, even if they were very different from hers, and so he feels secure in the belief that she is comfortable communicating with him.

Every Sunday, Leo sets aside time to go and sit in the garden in the front yard of his rental house. Six years ago, before she died, his mother had helped him plant the garden with cheerful teasing that the house needed a woman's touch. As Leo set up two lawn chairs in the garden and relaxed, he could already feel the stress draining out of his body. His shoulders lowered and his mind calmed, getting ready for the spiritual work he needed to do.

Leo pulled a crumpled piece of paper from his breast pocket. His mom was always the sort of person to make "to-do" lists on scraps of paper, so he always brought one along for spirit communication so he wouldn't forget anything important. Today's list, however, was full of things he knew he wouldn't forget. In messy penmanship, he'd scrawled "What does mom think of my girlfriend?," "What advice does mom have about buying a house?," and "Tell mom I love her."

Leo closed his eyes and squeezed the piece of paper tightly, feeling a connection to his mom in this little habit they shared. As the wind whispered through the garden, he could almost feel his mother take a seat in the empty lawn chair next to him, her legs brushing the tops of the flowers as she passed him. He smiled and kept his eyes closed, not wanting to let the moment of illusion that she was still alive to pass.

"Hi Mom," he murmured. "I miss you." He could sense her smiling as if the warmth of her joy radiated from her spirit.

"Mom, this might be the last time we meet here in the garden you planted for me," Leo admitted, "I put in an offer on a house I want to own. I'll plant a garden there to be sure, but it won't be the same." Leo fought the tears that he felt behind his eyelids, but one trickled out from a corner of his eye. He brushed it away, and noticed a curious warmth at his right shoulder. It was as if his mom's spirit was laying a comforting hand on him. In his mind, he could almost hear her voice saying "there, there" as she always used to do. She never tried to tell him that his feelings didn't matter; instead she had always said "there,

there" to direct his attention elsewhere, to the real blessings he had in life. He was certain in that instant that his mom would continue to meet with him even if it wasn't in the garden she planted. He brought her spirit everywhere with him in his heart.

"You never met Janice in life," he said, changing the subject to his girlfriend. "I'm thinking of proposing to her. Do you think she is right for me? Do you approve?" He could feel himself getting more nervous. In life, no girlfriend seemed good enough for him in his mom's eyes, but her perspective seemed to soften in her spirit form. Leo strained to hear or feel something from his mom, but she let him squirm a few moments longer, as she so often liked to do. Then, at once, an image flashed through his mind. A small, round, metal tin in the storage room, sitting underneath an old photo album. It had been filled with mom's old jewelry when he placed it in there. The ring! Leo suddenly realized that his mom was giving him the message to use her old engagement ring to propose.

Relief washed over Leo, and he sat quietly for a few minutes. The setting sun warmed his face, and the birds chirped as they chose their roosts for the night. In that instant, Leo felt that he was still cared for by his protective mother, that she was continuing to help him develop into the man she always wanted him to be. As he became more aware of his surroundings and the rumblings in his stomach reminding him that it was dinner time, Leo bid his mom goodbye once more, saying simply, "I love you." Then he went inside to prepare her favorite dinner.

Why do some spirits communicate while others do not? Much of that choice is up to the spirit itself. A spirit might choose to busy itself with the afterlife, be it a heavenly paradise, an alternate dimension, or reincarnation into an earthly body. However, a belief in heaven or reincarnation is not mutually exclusive to a belief in spirit communication. Souls have been known to divide their attention between an afterlife and their spirit communication with humans. It is also my understanding that spirits seem to experience time differently than living humans. This makes it possible for a person's soul to undergo reincarnation and spirit communication with seemingly paradoxical timing.

The number one reason I have heard a spirit tell me that he or she has not communicated with a loved one is out of a concern that it will affect the grieving process negatively or out of an assumption that the loved one would not want spirit communication. That's why you should bring up the subject of spirit communication with people in your life before you are a spirit. You might be surprised at how many people would love to hear from people who they miss dearly, or who are simply curious about spirit communication. Typically we call somebody who can talk to spirits a "psychic" or "medium," meaning that the person can sense things that aren't ordinarily perceived with the five senses. However, anyone can develop the ability to talk with spirits.

A spirit may choose to communicate immediately after death if there is unfinished business, such as identifying a murderer. More mundane unfinished business can appear as well. When I first contacted my dad's spirit after he died, his spirit had plenty to say about his material possessions, where certain sentimental treasures of his were hidden and what objects were supposed to be sold along with others as a set. So much for the classic, "I love you and am doing fine," sort of reassurances typically portrayed in movies.

Another reason for spirit communication may be to offer living people reassurance that there is life after death. Harry Houdini famously told his wife, Bess, a secret coded message in life that he, as a spirit, would say to her after death to prove it was his spirit communicating, and not just an enterprising fraudulent spirit communicator for hire. After making the pact, Houdini died in 1926, and his wife faithfully conducted séances once a year on Halloween for ten years. There are mixed reports given as to the success of the experiment, with a 1929 letter signed by Bess confirming that a psychic medium named Arthur Ford had communicated the exact message as well as how to decode it. However, she later refused to pay Ford some agreed upon prize money for the feat and continued to hold séances until giving up in 1936, reversing her claim and asking not to be contacted in the spirit world herself.

Finally, some spirits remain in their descendants' lives to enjoy a sense of eternal life through the memories of generations of new loved ones. Such spirits can choose to keep communicating to offer help and protection to the living. A little supernatural aid in achieving goals can go a long way and allow your loved ones who survive you to have successful lives as if by magic.

I want to communicate as a spirit after death to continue to aid and advise people. I also want my children and their children to always know that they are part of a loving family with a strong spiritual tradition. I can give them the gift in life of not treating death and spirits as taboo subjects. After I am gone, I can continue to be with them in spirit, if not in body. After all, a healthy and natural avoidance of dying is a good thing, but a crippling fear of death is not.

Developing a Tradition in Your Family That Celebrates Life and Ancestors

Getting over our cultural issues with life and death is easier said than done. Our attitudes towards death are a blessing and a curse. In modern times, death has been sanitized; we quickly whisk away bodies before many people see them. While it means we don't contract as many diseases from our dead as in old Europe where vigils were held for days to say goodbye or in ancient Egypt where mummies were propped up at the dinner table for special occasions, it means that many of us have never seen a dead person. The experience of being with a loved one during the dying process can be more traumatic than inspiring as a result.

Moving past the trauma of a loved one's death is the first step many of us have to take before starting spirit communication. If the last time you saw a deceased loved one was when that formerly strong person was languishing in a hospital bed, you may not want to summon those memories of that person to communicate. It may feel easier to just push all memories away and try to move on completely through denial and distraction. Spirit communication isn't about reliving the dying process, but about celebrating the wisdom and personality of the spirit's human life. And, of course, spirit communication is about seeking aid, wisdom, and comfort for the lives of those still living.

A Wake at Death

At the time of death, it may be impossible to avoid sadness. If it is your desire, there can be a solemn funeral to mark the occasion. In my family, however, instead of a funeral we like to celebrate with a wake. If you think of the cliché about a noisy party so loud it can "wake the dead," you'll have some idea about what a wake can be like. A wake, rather than being a formal ritual or ceremony at a funeral parlor or graveyard, is an informal celebration usually held in a home, although for my grandmother we held a boisterous wake in a restaurant.

At a wake, the details are not important, but it is understood that sadness, quiet, and solemnity are to be avoided. Instead, happy memories should be shared and stories should be told about the deceased, the more embarrassing and bawdy the better. At the typical wake there is much drinking and laughing. At the wakes I have attended, the atmosphere feels like the deceased is right there with us at a place of honor at the table, laughing at the stories and joining in with the libations.

Holidays

There's nothing more joyful than holidays, and paying attention to the darker side of holidays can be one way to recognize the cycle that starts with death and ends in rebirth. By celebrating the darker side, I don't mean having a solemn, scary, or sad holiday. Celebrating the darker side of holidays means acknowledging death, decay, and destruction as a part of nature, life, and their cycles.

Celebrating the idea of sacrifice in holidays reminds me that death is a sacrifice in order for life to exist. If every single human that ever lived still had a body here on earth, there would not be enough resources to sustain anything. We each will have to relinquish our bodies one day in order for our planet and our successors to flourish. Every day the sun has to set in order to rise again the next day. And every year, we have to kill our crops and livestock to harvest food to sustain life. One of those harvests is called Halloween, All Soul's Day, the Day of the Dead, or Samhain (pronounced "SOW-wen"). It is celebrated at the last night of October and first day of November.

One way I honor my ancestors during Samhain, just when the trees are sacrificing their leaves, is through a dumb feast. I make dishes that would have pleased my ancestors. A traditional food for the dumb feast is the pomegranate, but you can include recipes associated with your family or nationality to serve as well. During the dumb feast, incense is burned and those participating put a small sample of each food offered to the ancestors on a small plate. Then, we eat the rest quietly, not conversing among the living people present but listening quietly to perceive any messages from the ancestors whispered in our ears or appearing in the rising incense smoke. I always light a candle in front of a photograph of my dad propped up behind his watch so I can remember him and listen to what he would have to say around the dinner table.

The first Samhain after my father's death was very meaningful to me. I had already begun spirit communication with him, but the magic in the air around Samhain helped his communication feel clearer and closer than ever. Even though it took place six months after his death, I cried as if he had left his body the day before. I saw him very clearly that night and talked to him while he was in the room with me, hearing him speaking with me in turn. His presence in my house was so tangible that a friend of mine saw an apparition of him shortly thereafter, even though she is not given to seeing such things. It scared her at first, but then she realized that he was just protecting my home.

Another holiday, opposite in the year from Samhain is Beltane (also known as May Day), often celebrated on the last night of April or the first of May. On Beltane as on Samhain, it is said that the veil between the worlds is thin. I find that to be especially true for me since Beltane is when my father died. The night before his death, a priest had hugged me and whispered in my ear, "He will always be with you, he just won't be able to hug you like this." Through spirit communication, you can experience that comforting presence of your own loved ones as often as I do.

While Samhain is the time to come eye to eye with death, Beltane is the time of the year to reaffirm life, fertility, and abundance. Use your connection with the dead to ask them for aid with your family. Start a bonfire and gaze into that fire to see the eyes of your ancestors in the leaping flames. You can even pray for a bit of the spirit of a beloved relative who has passed to be reincarnated into the soul of a baby to be conceived in your family. Beltane is the joyous wake counterpart to the dirge that is Samhain. Both sides of death should be acknowledged and honored over the course of each year.

Celebrating with others, whether they are family or friends, can be a meaningful way to explore and reaffirm your faiths. I remember one particular Samhain during which I celebrated outdoors in nature with some close friends. Though we had a fire going for warmth, it is awfully cold in the Pacific Northwest on Samhain, so I huddled up in a hooded jacket. We all sang songs and then ate the traditional dumb feast. Incense was burning so thickly that the clouds of smoke resembled the wisps of wraiths, rising like ghosts in the atmosphere. One by one, members of the group took turns walking to an ancestor altar that burned brightly with candles. I continued to sit with my hood up around my ears, trying not to eavesdrop on what my friends were whispering at the altar, even though some of them sang and some of them wept.

All at once, in spite of myself, I couldn't help but look up because I could see the beloved spirits of the dead very clearly around the circle of people. The combination of my meditative state and the thick incense smoke multiplied those around the circle that night. I could see how the spirits interacted. Some of them seemed to lean forward and to whisper in the ears of the living. Others just sat quietly with their loved ones, holding hands. My own ancestors stood near me, and I could sense the emotion of pride emanating from them, which surprised me. In everyday life, chasing after my children and struggling through my daily chores it is hard to imagine my ancestors feeling that I am doing them proud. That Samhain night, however, I was able to feel some real perspective. I was proudly carrying forward my family's blood and memories, and my friends were doing the same in our shared fellowship. When it was my time to go to the altar, I did so gladly, throwing back the hood of my jacket to take in the beauty of the burning candles and the pictures of the smiling faces of our beloved dead.

Genealogy Research

I remember the first time I went to a ceremony held by a group that practiced Vodou, the Afro-Caribbean religion mentioned earlier, which celebrates and calls upon ancestors for help and advice. Those good folks knew how to include the dead in their holiday. Far from being a solemn occasion, there was much joy and plenty of people taking photos of the altar full of food offerings for ancestors for photo albums. This holiday was part of a living history of celebrating the dead.

I sat nervously, wondering if the *ghede*, the spirits of the dead with exaggerated personality characteristics that are often lewd or obscene, would possess anyone that night. Instead, I encountered joyous people who could name their family line all the way back to the diaspora from Africa via slavery. A woman would call out a name of a great, great, great grand-something-or-other and all would answer *ashe* in reply. I felt uncomfortable when my turn came to name dead relatives; most of my relatives were killed by Nazis and I didn't know their names. In fact, the closest dead people to me at the time of that ceremony were family, friends, and pets.

The leader of the Vodou ceremony grasped my shoulder kindly, finding the words I could not. "And to all those ancestors whose names we do not know" she said, "ashe!" As you bring the idea of honoring and celebrating the dead into your household, you may find that you want to know more about your family history, and that's a good sign. Even if your family members may not have believed in spirit communication while living, they most certainly loved their family enough to procreate. You are descended from a long line of love, known or unknown, and an interest in spirit communication is a great reason to begin researching your family tree.

If you don't know much or anything about your ancestors, or if some of that information is obscured or lost, consider doing a bit of your own genealogy research. Knowing the names and perhaps even finding photos and trivia about your ancestors can help you to connect with them and to feel that you belong to a lineage of memorable people. Your ancestors can help you with your goals in life, and they can support you in your quest to be heard after death. After all, if you want to be honored after you are dead, you should set a good example for those who may honor you by paying due tribute to your own ancestors.

In fact, members of the Church of Jesus Christ of Latter Day Saints have built and maintained an impressive number of genealogy records for spiritual purposes to offer baptism as a means of spirit communication after death. In this powerful form of spirit communication, Mormons witness to their blood ancestors after death, presenting them with a choice to follow their religion or to decline if they wish. Obviously they too believe that spirits can have an active spirit life, since they can even experience religious conversion long after death.

Just recently I heard a knock at the door. It was my friendly neighborhood Mormon missionaries, and they asked if they could sing me a song. They sang a beautiful hymn about how families will be together forever in the afterlife. In the Mormon faith tradition, marriages seal people together eternally and families will be together in Heaven after death. So for Mormons, if you have a nasty

Aunt Myrtle you hate hanging around, it is a good idea to patch things up with her right away because you're not ever going to get away from her, even after your life on earth is over. The Mormon missionaries told me about an ancestry research center that they had opened at their local ward of the Church of Jesus Christ of Latter Day Saints. There, anyone could come and use software and genealogy website memberships for free. I asked if I could come and see it immediately. One of them asked, "Do you like adventures?"

I do. I do, indeed.

I followed the young pair of gentlemen to their church building and we were all surprised to find that there was a class going on that evening on ancestry research. I was happy to use the resources and was surrounded by others who, despite being from different faiths, were also spiritually tied to their families. They wanted to connect with even distant family relations about whom they had never heard. I highly recommend these centers. They are a resource for everyone to use, even those with no ties to the Mormon faith and no desires to convert.

Doing my own research has been interesting and fun. Modern research tools such as those provided by these friends make the process feel intuitive. I have been able to view pictures of ancestors I've never seen before and even read some of their stories. These tidbits make it easier for me to recognize them if I happen to see their spirit forms during dreams or other spirit communications. Working with established databases also allows me to fill in my little place on the family tree. I feel so good about making sure that my information is clear, complete and accurate so that my descendants will be able to find me in the future. Making sure that your own records are easy to find and well connected to your family names and family tree is one way that you can leave behind a legacy to future generations who may be interested in spirit communication with their ancestors.

Ancestor Altar

An ancestor altar is a sort of shrine created to honor the images and preferences of one's ancestors. Traditionally, only ancestors related by blood are included in an ancestor altar in photographs or statues. Your ancestor altar should be placed in a prominent location in your home or business to demonstrate your pride in your heritage and to allow the ancestors to be a part of your life and to aid your success. Your ancestor altar can be a shelf or a table all to itself, or it can be a corner of a larger family altar upon which members of your household can place sacred objects, hopes, and wishes. My kids sometimes place small stones or plants on the altar. The stones tend to stay there indefinitely, and when the plants start to wilt I leave them outdoors somewhere as an offering to the ancestors and to my Gods.

You can leave it up all year if you are comfortable acknowledging death all the time, or you can break it out for special occasions like the month of Halloween or the death date of a loved one. Obviously, I keep mine within reach of my small children. I try to teach them that what is sacred is not a toy, but you can put yours out of reach of small children and pets for safety, especially if you chose to have lit candles or incense on your altar. Barring all safety issues, it's not a terrible sign if your altar is knocked down by an errant pet cat. Take it as an opportunity to dust off the altar, refresh any offerings and perhaps redecorate it for the season.

During Samhain, I build a temporary altar to my ancestors. I put up photographs in which I am careful to include only the deceased, cropping out images, if any, of those who are still living. A glass of water can be offered to the ancestors, along with any alcohol or food desired. One year I even offered a bit of the remainder of my dad's cologne, bringing back happy memories. Like the dumb feast, an ancestor altar can be reverent but also a labor of love and a source of fond reminiscence.

When you bring the dead from out of the shadows in the denial generated by our culture, then thinking about loved ones who have passed no longer has to be a solemn occasion. You can include the dark part of this cycle in daily life in a positive way, such as offering a little bit of each food to your ancestor altar at dinner. I am starting this tradition with my children on special occasions in the hopes that they will continue it into adulthood.

What do you do with the offered small bits of food after they have been ritually displayed on a tabletop offering

plate or at an altar or ancestral shrine? Place the food outdoors. It might seem a little irreverent to see local wildlife
or neighborhood pets finding and devouring the blessed
food, but they are acting in proxy for spirits. Death provides for life, as we all share the air, water, minerals and
other elements that were once in the bodies of those who
have gone before. Those little critters stealing a taste of
food from the offering plate may be your reincarnated
loved one, literally or figuratively.

Songs and games about death pepper my own childhood, and possibly yours as well. "Ring Around the Rosie,"
while possibly not actually representing people dying of
the black plague, is still a beautiful representation of the
cycle of life. Children dance in a circle, they fall down and
they get back up again. Singing songs from your childhood
around your ancestor altar can be one way to bring back
joyful memories, so much the better if they are songs and
games that your ancestors may also have played.

Shrine

An ancestor altar is one way to celebrate death, but you can
also set up a shrine for anyone who is not a blood relative.
For example, a shrine to a good friend who died. Many
cultures set up shrines to honor specific deities associated
with death, such as Kali in India, or Baron Samedi in Haiti.

You may even set up a shrine to honor a deceased pet.
Setting up a pet shrine is one way to help small children
understand death. You can set up the shrine briefly with

the child when the pet dies and keep it up for a week or a month, whatever seems appropriate for the child's age, or you can set up the pet shrine around Halloween to acknowledge the death of a pet for the child to remember.

When I was a kid, I built a shrine when my first dog died. The shrine consisted of a small table and a tiny brass statue of a dog, around which I placed her collar and a drawing I made of her. I kept the shrine there until I felt ready to let go and put things away in a memory box. You don't have to be a child to set up a pet shrine. A shrine can be a creative and constructive way to make the transition of death seem not so abrupt.

Stories

I don't directly remember much about Grandpa Nick in life. He died when I was a baby, and the only living memory of him that I have is that he and I shared a special wave, wiggling the fingers instead of the palm of the hand. As a shy person in life, his spirit is equally reserved and unlikely to make a big show when appearing. However, my parents told me many stories about my grandpa, and I have learned a great deal about his personality.

Before the days of television, storytelling was a family tradition, often done gathered around the hearth fire in the evening. It's not too late to revive that tradition with your own family and friends, and you certainly don't need a fireplace to do it. After dinner, switch off any electronic distractions and tell a few stories about those who have died before you, even if they are not blood relations. If you don't know any, do some genealogy research—you may stumble across exciting stories and pictures to share. The more you show the importance of continuing storytelling, the more likely people are going to share your own tales in the future.

Don't be afraid to start sharing your own stories now. Your family will love to hear fun stories from your childhood, and tales like how you and your significant other met and any birth stories of children can be told over and over again. Think about what achievements of yours are important for your family to remember. Will I want my loved ones to remember that I was the first person in our family to go to college, or do I want to share stories about the people I have helped? All of these can be starting points for fascinating tales that help reveal your values and universal truths in life that you have discovered during your journey on this earth.

Creating Bonds in Life to Last After Death

Creating holiday traditions and offering thankfully to ancestors at dinner isn't the only way to start cementing the eternal bonds between your family members. Remind your loved ones that you will always love them. It isn't enough to just think it, you have to say the words.

Consider how your beloved dead can be included in rites of passage in your life. My best friend had an extra bridesmaids chair at her wedding for her dead sister-in-law who was mentioned in the toasts. When I was getting married, I even included words in my vows with my husband that we would reconnect in another life, in forms pleasing to us, to know and love each other again. My priest was quite insistent about the "in forms pleasing to us" part. He didn't want my husband to be reborn as a frog in the next life to create some sort of tragic fairy tale. It's good to include themes of life and death in rites of passage in a positive way. By acknowledging reincarnation during my own marriage ceremony, my husband and I felt connected to the eternal, even in this finite lifetime.

As you move through rites of passage in your own life, think of ways to include the dead or the whole cycle of life, including the darker half. As a rite of passage when my father died, I got a memorial tattoo in his honor. You don't need ink on your skin to remember somebody for the rest of your life, but in order for your values to live after you do, you'll have to say some words about the matter that will stick in the minds of those who remain. Find opportunities to share the stories of your beloved dead with those around you, especially younger people. That way, they will share stories of you when you are gone.

Getting Your Act Together Before Dying

In some cases, I really believe that people can choose whether or not they are going to die. My dad was an insurance agent, and I heard countless stories from clients defying or meeting their deaths. In one case, the human body triumphed after an incredible wreck that by all means should have killed the driver. In another case, a driver hit a small bump in the road, the top of his head met the ceiling of his car very briefly and he died. I remember my own grandmother hanging onto life despite having several strokes and even being hit by a car at age eighty-six. I truly believe to this day that she decided to die because she didn't like the food at the hospital! Despite the amazing element of choice in the timing of your death, you might not be given the chance to make that choice if, say, a piano falls on your head, so it is important to make preparations before you're gone.

You can prevent your own loved ones from stressing about unfinished business after your own death by preparing as much as you can for the inevitable. When my father died, my family knew that it was coming for a long time. He had been given six months to live by his oncologist and then managed to live two years past that point. While we knew emotionally that it was going to happen, we lived our practical lives in denial. When he died there were many issues for my poor mother, his wife of thirty-five years, to resolve.

She didn't know any of his passwords to any accounts, and was unaware of the location of important documents. She would find keys to safety deposit boxes she had no idea existed. Every day new bills would come in the mail that were unexpected, since she hadn't been taking care of the family finances. In all of this she was also grieving, of course. Now you can imagine how much worse that entire process would have been if the death were entirely unexpected. Here is a compilation of some of the things he did right, and some of the things that we wish he would have done. I am no substitute for a lawyer or financial planner, so this information is here just to give you an idea of what plans to make. And yes, my husband and I have both made our plans with a lawyer, even though we are in our early thirties.

Mundane duties to address before death

- Take care of emotional unfinished business. Tie up loose ends. Make peace.

- Solidify your friendships. They will help take care of your family after you're gone.

- Live a meaningful life according to your values.

- Leave a legacy. Record memories in pictures, videos, and writing for your family.

- Make sure your family knows the details of your financial situation and budget.

  ○ Keep an emergency savings as well as a retirement savings.

- Get life insurance, short-term disability, and long-term disability insurance.

• Write a living will. This is different than a will because it covers decisions made while you are still alive but perhaps too ill or injured to express your wishes. The vast majority of people leave the earth in this slow way instead of a sudden death, so their family is forced to stress about end-of-life decisions.

  ○ Your living will should have medical power of attorney, the person who will be calling all the shots about your care while you are unable to do so.

  ○ Advance directives—Would you want the plug pulled if you were in a vegetative state?

  ○ How would you want to spend your last terminally ill days? In a hospice? At home?

  ○ Do you want your organs donated? Do you prefer burial or cremation?

  ○ Do you have any special requests for your funeral, memorial, or wake?

  ○ Give your doctor an updated copy of your living will and tell your family your wishes.

• Write a will and have it notarized and signed. Tell people where an updated copy is located.

  ○ Your will should include financial and medical durable power of attorney. That means you should list people who can make decisions for you and your dependents when you are incapacitated. Make sure to discuss it with that person and pick backup people just in case.

- ◦ Your will should list who will take custody of any children, if you and your spouse are both killed in the same accident, for instance. List backup people as well.

- ◦ Who will get property, personal treasures, and other assets? Who would you want to be in charge of the messy business of distributing all that stuff?

- Write down what accounts you own and all passwords for joint accounts somewhere safe.

- Consider creating a trust for your children if you have many or varied assets.

- Check all the above periodically, especially after major life events like a death, a birth, a marriage or a divorce. Your decisions may change.

Healthy Spirit Communication: Letting Go and Moving On Without Forgetting

How can you make spirit communication a healthy part of your life without dressing in black and getting stuck on thoughts of death and the past? By looking to the future, of course. If you have recently lost somebody, you will naturally need to find some closure. My first communications with my dad were filled with messages he had about where he had put things and attempts to get his material objects in order so my mother could sell them. Your spirit communications may include a lot of unfinished business, goodbyes, apologies, and regrets. But as time progresses, you will hopefully begin to treat your deceased loved one as just another important person in your life who happens to live on a different plane of existence.

If you find yourself obsessed with death and unable to live your life normally out of fear of death or regrets about the deceased, it may be time to discuss your feelings further with a counselor. The balance, that is, including the spirit world in everyday living, is possible. Everything in life changes, and you should progress towards those transitions with the help and loving support of your loved ones with whom you communicate in the spirit world. In chapter 4, we'll explore how you can prepare for your own transition into an everlasting persona in the spirit world in a matter-of-fact yet exciting way.

Things to Consider

1. What do you fear most about death and why? What life experiences have altered your perceptions of death as you progressed from childhood towards adulthood and beyond?

2. How does death usually touch your life? Do you have regular rituals or prayers to the dead, or do you normally just hear about death on the evening news? What are some ways you can add positive associations with death to your life?

3. Think about somebody you know who has died. How have your feelings changed for the better over time as you've been moving through the grief process. Do you feel that person is at peace? Do you feel that person's spirit with you from time to time? If so, how do you know?

4. What do you think the experience is like for the spirit immediately after death? What about twenty years after death?

5. How do you think the dead feel about life? What do you think their attitudes are towards the living? How do you think you'll feel after you're gone?

CHAPTER TWO

Spirit Communication With Loved Ones— A Crash Course

Spirit communication is a practice that has been with us since the beginning of human history. Many techniques are available. Methods range from simply talking aloud, believing that spirits are in the same room as you and listening at the time, to elaborate rituals and ceremonies. Entire books can easily be written on one aspect of spirit communication alone, so what you'll find here are distilled essentials.

Starting with basic techniques that should be used in all spirit communications, we'll give you a survey of different methods of talking with spirits so you can choose one or more to practice. I'll give some generalized steps for practicing spirit communication while you're still alive. Finally, I'll put it all together with my own example, so that you can see all the detailed steps for a spirit communication session in one place, so that you can better see how your own instructions will play out.

To use this chapter most effectively, read through it once on your own. As you read, pick at least one spirit communication method that appeals to you. After you're through with the chapter, pick at least one loved one with whom you would love to continue a relationship after your death. If you want, you can even throw a spirit communication party. I've thrown countless spirit board (Ouija board) parties myself, and they can be a fun way to bond with people and to break the ice about spiritual topics. Gather together in the spirit of curiosity and love to try out some of the methods for yourselves. And remember that practice makes perfect.

What Does the Presence of a Ghost Look and Feel Like?

My two-year-old ran to me while I was doing chores in the living room one day and clung to my leg. "I'm scared of the ghost in the kitchen," she told me.

I dutifully sat down so she could climb into my lap. "How do you know it was a ghost," I asked.

"He told me he was a ghost!" she said excitedly.

I smiled, thinking about the dead people I know who might self-identify as ghosts to a toddler. "Well," I started slowly, "what did he look like?"

"He was tall," my daughter began, which didn't really narrow things down because everybody is tall to a toddler. "He had hair on his face," she pointed to the area just under her little nose. "And he tried to hug me!" she pouted.

It sounded a lot like my dad to me, so I told her, "I think that might just be your Grandpa Roy? You know, it's okay to tell him if you don't want a hug. You don't have to be scared of ghosts."

"Okay," she agreed, hopping out of my lap. "I don't have to be scared. I will tell him." She raced off to the kitchen and I giggled as I heard her loudly proclaiming that, "I just don't want to be hugged by ghosts right now!" She came back into the living room beaming and told me. "It's okay. He will just watch until I am ready."

Before we get into the specifics of calling up ghosts, I'd like to go over some of the signs of spirit presence in case they are already happening to you before you begin summoning. Educating those around you about these signs can be a good way to acclimate them to the idea of your presence lasting after you are gone. The presence of a ghost can be as dramatic as a humanoid apparition or it can be as subtle as a feeling or memory. Here are a few signs that your loved ones may still be around.

Finding white feathers is one curious legend of spirit presence. Perhaps because they are associated with angel wings and because they are light and easy to move, spirits may be able to deposit or float white feathers to their loved ones. I have heard stories of friends who sat in graveyards paying their respects to loved ones and found the mysterious presence of white feathers floating down with no birds in sight.

A physical feeling of coldness, an inexplicable emotional feeling or a sudden flood of memories can also signify the presence of a ghost for some people. These senses may be in conjunction with other clues, or they may come independently. These clues are more subtle, so you will have to judge them in accordance with your personality. For example, if you're the type of person who rarely gets outwardly emotional, it would be unusual to suddenly be struck with emotional memories and start crying. Likewise, there's nothing much out there that scares me, and I'm generally not an anxious person, so if I get spooked it is usually as the result of a spooky ghost.

Shadows in peripheral vision, a feeling of being watched, or a vague sense that somebody is in the room are other subtle spirit perceptions. You can help focus those feelings by asking the spirit to stand in front of you. These perceptions can also be used to begin identifying spirits. For example, by saying, "if you are the spirit of my mother, please stand at my left shoulder. If you are the spirit of my father, please stand at my right shoulder."

Ghost Appearances

Some people such as myself see ghosts not only in dreams or behind closed eyelids, but right in front of their eyes. You may wonder then why some people describe ghosts differently than others. There's no way to know for sure whether ghosts take certain forms and patterns, or whether the patterns are ingrained within the viewers by culture and perception. I suspect the latter is true. However, here are a few very common forms for which you can watch.

Ancestral ghosts—These ghosts take the form of departed family members, so you might recognize them as taking the form of the person they were in life.

Animal ghosts—Animals can be ghosts as well, so a dearly departed pet or the ghost of some local wildlife might appear before you in a vision.

Apparitions—This can be a catch-all term for all ghost sightings solid or transparent. Crisis apparitions are a type that replay a scene of crisis experienced during life.

Banshee—A ghost that appears as a female who is wailing a mourning cry. The banshee is supposed to foretell a death.

Battlefield ghosts—If you want to see ghosts, you might want to head to a battlefield, which is a common place to see uniformed apparitions.

Celebrity ghosts—Ghosts of favorite celebrities are often summoned at séances and Spirit Board parties. There are some hotels and other tourist locations at which celebrity ghost sightings are common and always seem to take the same form.

Ectoplasm—A white substance that may appear during séance sessions.

Energy lines—Most often appearing in photographs as a white lightning bolt mark, these white lines are supposedly the visible energy of ghosts.

Fairies—There are those who believe that myths and legends about fairies are derived from ghost sightings. Fairies take many forms, but the classic fairy shape is often a little person who may or may not be winged or nude.

Fetch—This looks like an exact duplicate of a person, a doppelgänger, and is seen just before the person is to die.

Ghoul—These appear as emaciated humans or zombies. They are usually found only in graveyards.

Historic ghosts—When I go traveling to historic places, I keep a lookout for significant ghosts of the location. Certainly a given place may be the habitat for the ghosts of anyone who has ever lived there, but you can try to identify a crisis apparition of a historical figure by its garb, actions, and face.

Incubus—A male ghost that may appear demonic and seduces sleeping women to drain their energy.

Inhuman object ghosts—A ghost ship, ghost train, or ghost plane fits into the category of ghost objects. These may appear to be animated, and can be translucent or solid.

Living ghosts—This is actually the soul or astral form of a person who is still alive. Astral means that the ghost does not exist physically, but rather in a spiritual place that you can reach in your mind through visualization or dreams. For example, when you sleep or meditate in a trance, an image that may appear as an outline of yourself can be seen traveling outside of your body.

Monsters—Malformed animals or demonic beasts might be ghosts taking a terrifying form to scare the living or as a symbol of its tormented emotional state.

Nature ghosts—When some natural spots are destroyed by people, nature ghosts may manifest as angry beings. These may appear similar to fairy people, or they can take the form of ghost trees that are inhabited by spirits but appear to be ordinary trees.

Orbs—These balls of light may appear in photographs, but a clairvoyant may also be able to see them floating around.

Poltergeists—Poltergeists are invisible, but they are made visible by their activities. So, for example, a floating dress may actually be a poltergeist.

Possessive ghosts—These ghosts may be invisible, but they make themselves visible by going inside the body of a living person and using his or her body to speak and move.

Shadow ghosts—Ghosts that appear as a dark mist or a shadowy outline of a human form are shadow ghosts. Features will not be discernible. These ghosts most often appear at night.

Spirit guides—Guardian ghosts are a category under which spirit guides and guardian angels may fall. Some people may see them as angelic figures with wings, while others may see them take the form of a human. In early Spiritualism days, the figure of a wise old Native American was a common form, for example. A spirit guide may follow you for a lifetime, or may trade off with other spirit guides during specific life phases. To meet your spirit guide, you can travel through the astral plane (mentally induced spiritual landscape) or during a dream to his or her home. To find out the name of your spirit guide, you can simply ask him or her when present, and your spirit guide will tell you or spell it out for you in some way.

Succubus—A female ghost that may appear demonic
 who seduces sleeping humans to drain their energy.

Wraith—Appears as a tall, gaunt humanoid form wearing
 a black or white shroud that obscures the face. A
 wraith is supposedly an omen that foretells death.

I have seen several forms of the above ghosts, though
not all of them. And I have also seen some forms that I
have never seen described anywhere else. One ghost, for
example, I saw in the living room of my old house years
ago, though the experience is so vivid and strange now that
I can easily admit that it may have been a dream. The ghost
drifted slowly through a wall out of nowhere, and it appeared human, yet its face seemed to shift. Over the course
of a minute, its face and other physical features shifted
smoothly but quickly, as if a Technicolor light illuminated
different people existing in one form.

I spoke with the ghost, and it told me that it was essentially an amalgam of many joined spirits. I asked where
it was coming from and where it was going. It had recently
picked up a new spirit and was drifting slowly to the next
location in which a spirit would join the amalgam. As it
glided through the wall as quickly as it came, I imagined
rain drops on a windshield, each joining one another until
they were heavy enough to slide into a rivulet of flowing
runoff, to one day begin the water cycle anew.

How will you know who it is?

Some of the signs associated with spirits are specific to a particular person. This can be helpful to you, if you want to identify the spirit, and helpful for preparing your loved ones for interacting with you on the other side if you want to set up a sign for your loved ones to anticipate.

Finding objects that are associated with a specific person can be interpreted as a sign. For example, finding marbles all over the house if the person in question enjoyed playing with marbles during life. Whenever I find a penny, I think about my dad. He always made a huge ruckus out of finding lucky pennies on the ground, and he had an eagle eye for them. Once, he dove into some bushes to the side of a path and retrieved a penny that didn't even seem to be visible. We joked about him having a nose for money. When my father's spirit was leaving his body, before I was even ready to attempt spirit communication with him, I found a penny and took it as a sign from him.

Scents associated with a specific person bring back instant memories, and can seem to materialize literally out of thin air. Follow your nose if you sense perfume or cologne that was associated with a loved one in life. This may vary for different people, even in the same environment. I tend to smell my dad's cologne when his spirit is around, while my mom smells his cigarette smoke. He probably knows that I would be annoyed at cigarette smoke since I never approved of his smoking in life.

And finally, the best way to know that a spirit has come is to summon a specific spirit by name, which will be described later in this chapter. But how do you make sure the right spirit arrived? Or what if a spirit has come without any clues as to its identity? There is lore that a spirit cannot sign any name but its own. Present the spirit with a way to write its name, such as a Spirit Board, a writing implement with paper and a person to perform automatic writing, or a mirror on which a person breathes condensation. In my experience, spirits do have the ability to garble names, or to give their identity as a nickname like "devil" or "boy." That can be just as confusing as lying. So, again, the best way to identify spirits is to be really specific when summoning them.

What is Talking With a Ghost Like?

I wasn't always such a brave spirit communicator. When I was a child, I was scared of ghosts, just like every other kid I knew. At Halloween, ghost stories were told, and we all waited with anticipation for skeletal apparitions to burst forth from the darkness of hallways in my house. Thankfully, they never did. When kids dressed up as ghosts for trick-or-treating, sometimes they'd paint blood on top of white makeup, which made me look away in disgust and fear. Ghosts in movies would change shape suddenly, which made me leave the room for scary scenes and ask my mother to let me know when it was all over. I was also quite certain that a ghost lived in my basement, so I ran up the stairs extra fast after turning out the light.

I was still quite young when my grandma died, and to the best of my recollection, she may be the first spirit of a family member I remember seeing specifically. She waited until the night time to appear and then moved about the house as a dark figure pushing the vacuum cleaner, of all things. You wouldn't think that a ghostly grandma cleaning the house would be too terrifying as far as the spectrum of deathly visages is concerned, but it frightened me to fits of insomnia. Of course, at that age, any person who looked different was scary to me, even the living elderly or the disabled. It took me some time to get used to the idea that people are people, even if they look different, and that a spirit form is just another way to be human.

Having a conversation with a ghost these days is always pleasant to me, and sometimes exciting. Even though I have practiced long and frequently enough to be able to hear some spirits as if they were talking in the same room with me, the communication is not always so obvious. Sometimes sensing the presence is very subtle as described in the section above. Sometimes I choose to use divination techniques (described later in this chapter) to amplify and clarify the ghostly presence into an actual message. At one point in my life I was interviewed by a forensic researcher who was trying to puzzle out how psychics might one day be used by law enforcement professionals. He had noticed that in some cases spirits are more silent than others, regardless of which psychic is used.

The difference between ghostly communication experiences sometimes has to do with the person communicating, but it often has to do with the message being communicated and with the ghost's personality. For example, my deceased Grandma Bessie and Uncle Ronny were extremely loud-mouthed and loquacious in life, so it only makes sense that their communications to me after death are equally free-flowing. Meanwhile, more shy and quiet people in life, like my Grandpa Nick, remain a more fleeting presence in death. I am sure that I will be quite talkative to everyone after death, but if you tend to be shy and reserved, this correlation may be something to mention to your living relatives so they aren't discouraged when more attempts are needed to communicate.

Grounding and Centering

The most important skill to learn before practicing spirit communication is grounding and centering. Grounding and centering is a process by which you connect with the present moment as well as the earth to feel balanced, calm, and healthy. Without proper grounding, spirit communication can be energetically and emotionally flustering or draining, especially in the early grieving period right after a loss. It is important for you and your loved ones to practice grounding and centering now so it will be an automatic resource to which you can turn later on. Besides, grounding can also be helpful in your everyday life if you ever feel too jittery, too amped up on anxious energies, or lethargic and lacking proper energy to function.

Visual Grounding

Grounding and centering can be achieved through simple visualization and self-talk. Begin by going to a place with few distractions so you can focus on what you sense inside your mind and body. Sit comfortably and close your eyes, tuning in to your body sensations. You might want to focus on your breathing or heart rate for a few moments to calm yourself and to begin to ignore the distractions of any sounds around you.

Turn your attention to your body and how you feel energetically. Do you feel tense, anxious, and jittery, or do you feel sluggish and exhausted? Try to pinpoint that feeling as a picture in your mind's eye, like a colored light or a concrete sensation in your body such as fizziness or buzzing. The visual or sensory representation is the energy you use to talk with spirits and do many other things in life. Next, you are going to get rid of the excess or negative energy and replenish your body with fresh energy from the earth.

Start by pushing the energy down and out of your body through your feet. It can help the beginner and expert alike if you are barefoot, but don't worry if there are physical barriers between you and the earth. Energy can travel through a high-rise building and you can even ground on an airplane. Make sure that you push out any excess energy that might make you too wired or that could carry negative emotions. Next, draw fresh energy up from the earth, sensing it in the same manner that you did your own energy. So if you saw a colored light for example, you might see a brighter and more vibrant light coming back up into your body. It is all right if the way you sense energy is different from these examples. The point of the exercise is to discover your own personal perspective and use it to successfully ground yourself.

When you are finished drawing energy from the earth, you should feel calm, relaxed, and also awake and ready for action. It takes practice to achieve a properly grounded state, because if you are still unbalanced you might find yourself feeling either hyper or sleepy. Keep practicing and you'll more quickly and accurately hit that sweet spot and be perfectly grounded. Always ground yourself before and after spirit communication to feel sustained and energetic throughout and afterward.

Tactile Grounding

Some people just aren't visual, and that's okay. You don't have to see energy in order to work with it. In fact, perceiving energy as a feeling can be very powerful. Tibetan Buddhist monks have been able to meditate perfectly still in freezing temperatures without experiencing hypothermia using the same energy that we draw up during grounding to raise their core body temperatures. A man named Wim Hof, using similar techniques, has run around the Arctic Circle barefoot and nearly nude, and he hiked on Mount Everest similarly unequipped against the cold. He has set twenty world records for miracles such as meditating in baths of ice water, and now he teaches his method far and wide in an effort to share the magic. Here is the method, which requires no visualization:

Rest and close your eyes, either in a seated position or lying down. Begin taking deep breaths. (The Wim Hof method uses several deep breathing techniques, so you should make sure you are seated or lying down somewhere safe in case you feel light headed.) These breaths should be deep, from your diaphragm, and they should fill your whole lungs. Take your time, breathe slowly, and hold for an instant before exhaling. You should take about fifteen of these deep, slow breaths to warm up for the grounding.

When you feel relaxed, you will change your breathing pattern to a series of about thirty power breaths. Power breaths are also deep, but more forceful, as if you are blowing up a balloon, breathing in through your nose and out through your mouth. You can perform these more quickly and without pause, but you might feel light headed and tingly, so make sure you are lying down or seated somewhere safe. As you perform these power breaths, take an inventory of your body sensations to feel for negative energy to be purged with these power breaths. Such energy might feel like tiredness, coldness, constriction, or another negative feeling. Let the power breaths push it all away and try to replace those sensations with warm energy.

Next, to draw in more warm energy, you will return to taking a couple of deep, slow breaths. Fill your lungs as much as you can, breathe out, and then hold your breath for a bit. When your lungs tell you they need to breathe again, take another deep breath and this time hold your breath with the air filling your lungs, hopefully for about ten to fifteen seconds if you can (less is okay if you are unable to do so.) As you perform this last hold, take another inventory of your body and send energy in the form of heat to any places that seem to need it. The process is meant to be repeated, so if you feel like you need to do it again, try a second round or more.

Kinesthetic Grounding

Here is another method of grounding that is more kinesthetic than tactile or visual, that means that it involves moving your body with a practice until it is done. You still have to feel when you are grounded, but it may be simpler for beginners than other methods. Since I am a dancer, I like to use this method to loosen myself up before dancing as well. It may look ridiculous, but it sure works!

This method is performed standing in one place. You may close your eyes if you can, but if you feel like you need your eyes open to keep your balance, that's okay too. Wiggle and shake your body to rid yourself of negative energy. As you do so, take an inventory of what parts of your body may not be shaking as much due to tight muscles.

Move from head to toe, making sure that you shake out all parts of your body. Be careful with your head, as you don't want to damage your neck with whiplash. I tend to drop my chin to my chest and relax my neck and face, letting my head bob gently as I shake but not whipping it around. I like to shrug my shoulders and let them drop repeatedly to release the tension. Shake your hands as if you are shaking off water droplets. Stomp your feet in place on the ground. Let your feet stomping send jolts of jerky energy back up into your body so that the movement reverberates to your fingertips.

Ideally, you should perform this shaking for a good period of time, at least five minutes, and I like to do it for fifteen whole minutes. The purpose is to get past the awkwardness of the movement and to let it work its grounding magic, letting your muscles get tired of bracing against your own movement so that you will truly relax. Just as you have to hold a stretch to relax, this shaking energy requires the investment of some time.

Centering

After you're finished grounding, it is time to center yourself. Sit quietly with your eyes closed and bring your attention back to the present moment. If your mind has wandered to anxieties about the past or worries about the future, bring it back on task and check in with your emotions. Are you ready to communicate with spirits at this time? If there is a specific spirit with whom you wish to talk, are you truly prepared for a confrontation? Are you ready to hear news of any sort from the afterlife, possibly about your past, present, and future? If you're feeling in the least bit emotionally vulnerable, you may wish to wait so your spirit communication doesn't interfere with your grief process or with the way that you are living your life. If the time is right, you should feel calm, relaxed, alert, optimistic, and strong.

Prepare for Spirit Communication: A Sacred Space

Have you ever been in a place that just seemed magical and holy, such as a church or a stone circle? I've been to Stonehenge, Knowth, and Newgrange; the experiences were amazing. My mother was lucky enough to win a lottery allowing us to be inside the sacred chamber at the stone structure. On the morning of the winter solstice, the light of the sunrise pierces the chamber of Newgrange with a line that shines along the back wall.

We shivered inside a human-made cave in the complete darkness with about a dozen strangers, waiting for the moment to arrive. As the sun rose and a golden ribbon sliced across the seemingly infinite blackness, the holiness of the place brought me to tears. I imagined what it would be like to be there thousands of years ago to see the same sight. The people in the inner chamber with us reached out towards the light. We all bathed our hands in it and waved glittering jewelry in the light, begging the magic of the space to bless it.

There's no way to completely reenact the experience of being in a famous holy location, but you can create sacred space wherever you like. Any place in the world can be your church as long as you put yourself in the right state of mind. The point of creating sacred space for spirit communication is twofold. Firstly, sacred space helps welcome the spirit, as you would want your special reunion to happen in a special place. Secondly, sacred space helps to protect you from any influences that you don't want to affect you while you are performing spirit communication. The creation of a sacred space can repel malicious entities and even quell negative emotions that you might otherwise experience. Here are some simple steps to creating a temporary sacred space, outdoors, indoors, anywhere you like.

Step 1) After grounding and centering, cleanse the space. Some sweep with a broom, others simply visualize all negativity leaving the space in the same way one visualizes that energy during grounding. As with grounding, it can melt harmlessly into the earth to be transformed and reused as positive energy.

Step 2) Optionally, you can bless the area with incense. Frankincense is a good blessing incense, as is a sage smudge bundle. Walk around the space in a circle with the incense to invite blessing. Some choose to walk the circle three times clockwise for good measure. Visualization can be used here, especially in the absence of incense. This time, instead of ridding the area of energy, visualize a boundary forming with energy. Some people imagine a bubble, other people pretend that a tent is being set up around the area.

Or, you can simply draw a circle around yourself with your mind. The point of this boundary is to protect yourself from any spirits you don't want to visit while allowing the sacred space to be welcoming to the spirit you wish to call.

Step 3) Optionally, you may light candles at this time. Black candles are good for protection; white candles are good for blessing. Some people choose to light a candle in each of the four compass points to welcome blessings from all four corners of the earth. You can also choose a candle to represent the spirit with whom you are trying to communicate, especially if you know what that person's favorite color was during life.

Step 4) Pray. If you believe in a higher power, gods, or goddesses, at this point it is appropriate to pray to your source of divinity to invite protection and a loving presence. If you are new to prayer, or to feeling comfortable with prayer, I can provide you a brief sample here. I like to use the mnemonic of the letters in the word "PRAYING" for this formula which stands for: Person listening, Raise praise, Ask for help, Your deadline, Imperatives for safety, Note of thanks, and Gracious attention.

PERSON LISTENING
I invoke [God(s)/Goddess(es)/Spirit/
Universe/my Higher Self/etc.].

RAISE PRAISE
You who is/are the provender of all spirits
and the source of all communion.

ASK FOR HELP
Thank you for aiding spirit
communication and protecting me.

YOUR DEADLINE
Now.

IMPERATIVES FOR SAFETY
With harm to none, and for the
highest good of all. So may it be.

NOTE OF THANKS
In return, I offer you [Love, willingness
to spread the communicated message, etc.].

GRACIOUS ATTENTION
Blessed be. (Meditate and then reflect
on how you felt during and after.)

You are now ready to summon your spirit. Talk however long you wish, and then thank the spirit and allow it to leave. Since you are practicing for spirit communication with a specific person, I recommend only calling one spirit per session.

Don't forget to write down any messages received during spirit communication. The simple act of creating sacred space may induce a trance state in many people causing them to forget what happened in the sacred space in the same way that one forgets dreams. If you want to take those messages out into your everyday life, it would be best to write them down.

After Spirit Communication

Having thanked and said goodbye to the spirit you summoned, you can again bless the area with incense. It is an especially good time to use a sage smudge after your spirit communication session to cleanse the area of negativity and rid the space of any unwanted extra energy. Think of those big clouds of sage smoke as a chalkboard eraser, wiping the slate clean until next time. If you walked clockwise to prepare for spirit communication, it is proper to walk counterclockwise afterwards, cleaning up in the opposite manner in which you set up the space.

Ground yourself thoroughly. You may then clean up any of the tools you may have used during your spirit communication, extinguish any candles, placing any food or beverage offerings outdoors for wildlife to eat in proxy of the spirit called. This is a good reason to only include a token amount of food or beverages, so the wildlife won't get overly enthusiastic about your offerings.

Now that you have the preparation and an idea of what somebody's final wishes might be, you have all the ingredients for spirit communication. Now I'll flesh out your knowledge and put the filling in this sandwich—the particulars of spirit communication. Go ahead and try out one or more of these methods with your loved ones while you are both still alive so you can more easily find one that is simple and fulfilling enough for all concerned. You might even be able to get some good connections with deceased mutual friends out of your practice sessions. At the end of this chapter, I'll show you complete example instructions from an entire spirit communication session, start to finish.

Prayer

I use prayer every day to communicate with my gods and ancestors. It makes asking the deceased for advice as simple as calling somebody from the next room to talk to me. Often I will go to a spirit with a concern in the same way I would have in life. For example, when I bought my house, I took a moment to go privately where I could pray out loud to my dad and ask his advice. He was always pretty smart about money matters. I received encouraging words from him as an answer in my mind, "hearing" his voice in the same way I might hear a song stuck in my head. That short little conversation was enough to give me the boost I needed to buy the house without anxiety.

By far, the simplest method of spirit communication for some people is prayer. Prayer can be just speaking aloud to a spirit as you might speak aloud to a living person. In ancient cultures, ancestors were often consulted this way and were an active part of family life. One might speak aloud or pray to ancestors while doing household chores, such as sweeping the floor or washing dishes. Ancestors would be acknowledged through words and small gestures upon entering or leaving a home. For minimalists, prayer is a powerful and simple way to reestablish a relationship with a departed loved one.

As before, if you're new to prayer or feel a little uncomfortable and rusty getting started, you can use a simple prayer formula to give you an idea of the order of topics you can bring up with a loved one. The prayer can be as simple as to ask for communication from your loved one, as in this following example:

PERSON LISTENING
I invoke [name of spirit].

RAISE PRAISE
You who are [name three good things about the person in life].

ASK FOR HELP
Thank you for talking to me through [a feeling in my heart, a voice in my mind, the divination method of your choice, etc.].

YOUR DEADLINE
Now.

IMPERATIVES FOR SAFETY
With harm to none, and for the highest good of all. So may it be.

NOTE OF THANKS
*In return, I offer you [love, willingness
to spread the communicated message, etc.].*

GRACIOUS ATTENTION
*Blessed be. (Meditate and then reflect
on how you felt during and after.)*

Some people feel uncomfortable praying directly to ancestors without a deity or deities as mediators, and that's just fine. You can simply use the prayer that you used during your preparation for spirit communication to address the source of divinity of your choice to relay a spirit's message. There's no reason why you should have to push your comfort zone too far when praying, that's why it is a good idea to agree upon the prayer first if you are praying with more than one person in the room. If you get together with a family member or friend who wants to try out spirit communication, ask the person first whether it is okay that you say a prayer directly to the deceased. Likewise, if you say a prayer to your higher power, make sure it is okay with everyone present. Some belief systems don't play well with others, so a silent prayer time might be more appropriate in those instances to keep a harmonious atmosphere.

The best thing about using prayer for communication is that it is simple and doesn't require any extra time commitments, tools, or effort. The bad news is that not everyone receives a noticeable answer through prayer. Some people are not naturally sensitive enough to see and hear ghosts, and the skills of perceiving such messages can take time and effort to develop. Such people who use prayer and expect to get immediate results might feel disappointed or even abandoned by their spirit ancestors. If you choose to use prayer as a way to get in touch with spirits, try to detach yourself from the outcome and just pray out of the joy and fulfillment you get from speaking your message to the spirit, not from the answers you hope to receive.

Dreams

In dreams I have hugged my deceased grandmother and spoken with her in English even though she lost most of her English after a stroke. In a dream I've heard stories from my deceased uncle and I've gone traveling across the world with my dad's spirit, having him point out sights for me to see in countries I haven't yet visited. In dreams I have even been able to play with old dogs I have missed after many years since their deaths. The spirit communication doesn't have to happen right there during the spirit communication session on Halloween, or standing on a bridge over a river or whatever circumstances a spirit enjoys. You can use that invocation moment as a way to open a door between the two of you to invite the spirit to visit you in a dream or a series of dreams. Simply change the prayer to a dream appearance request like this:

PERSON LISTENING
I invoke [name of spirit].

RAISE PRAISE
*You who are [name three good
things about the person in life].*

ASK FOR HELP
Thank you for coming to visit me in a dream.

YOUR DEADLINE
*[tonight/by the next full moon/
any time you like/etc.].*

IMPERATIVES FOR SAFETY
*With harm to none, and for the
highest good of all. So may it be.*

NOTE OF THANKS
*In return, I offer you [love, willingness
to spread the communicated message, etc.].*

GRACIOUS ATTENTION
*Blessed be. (Meditate and then reflect
on how you felt during and after.)*

The hardest part about dream communication is remembering the dream as soon as you wake up. Trust me, no matter how mind-blowing and fulfilling the dream, even if tears are streaming down from your face upon waking from the memories of hugging your dear ones, you might forget the particulars a mere hour later. This is because your brain is in a special state when you first awaken. It is producing alpha waves, similar to those produced during meditation, instead of the beta waves associated with being fully alert and shifting memories from short-term to long-term.

The only solution is to record your dreams in a dream journal the instant you wake up. There is no way to train your brain to remember your dreams otherwise. That means that before showering or brushing your teeth, before nodding back off to sleep and even before getting out of bed, you should record your dreams in a dream journal. Have pen, paper, and a light by your bed so you can accomplish your task, and warn anyone who shares your bed or your room that you will be switching on a light to record your dreams, even if it is the middle of the night.

The hardest part about using dreams to communicate with spirits is that this sort of physical and mental challenge takes discipline. As soon as you wake up, you usually want to go right back to sleep or to get started with your day, not undertake a writing project. However, dream communication is accessible to anyone, even those who don't feel they have any natural spirit communication ability. Dreaming feels safe, because you only dream when you are asleep and not when you wake up, so you don't have to worry about seeing a ghost during your everyday waking life if that idea scares you. Best of all, dreams can feel just like real life, so an embrace with a loved one can feel the same as it did when he or she was alive. When I was able to hug my father in a dream after he died, I remember how tangible it felt.

Meditation

Meditation is challenging. Clearing your mind to allow messages from spirit to seep into the space between thoughts is much harder to do than it sounds. However, your discipline in meditation can be richly rewarding. Now that I am experienced in meditation, I can sink into a meditative state quite quickly, instead of fighting my brain for minutes on end. Once I am in the right headspace, I can experience a chat with my dad or my grandpa as if I were dreaming while still awake. When I first started meditation, however, it was hard. I spent every moment of it fighting my brain so hard I was surprised I didn't break a sweat. I was exhausted when I looked at the clock and saw only a few minutes had passed. It's okay if you feel this level of frustration at first, too! Keep working on meditation and it can become easier and more effective for you.

Meditation, when combined with prayer, is my go-to method for communicating with the spirits of loved ones. When talking with the spirits of strangers I often want to add another form of divination, since I don't know what they look like and don't want my imagination to run amok. But since the faces of my loved ones are always in my heart and mind the moment I close my eyes, meditation is a wonderful way to review those old memories and to begin to make some new ones.

In this section, I will explain how to meditate, but first I'd like to describe what it is like for an experienced medium to communicate with spirits through meditation. I know that for a beginner, it is hard to imagine meditation as anything more than just sitting still and getting bored. However, after you are practiced enough to allow your brain to slip into this state easily, you will experience something like lucid dreaming. This process makes your brain an empty slate upon which spirits can write or draw anything they want, allowing you to go on journeys to strange new astral planes; in other words, mental places. Unlike most dreams, however, you still have full control over what you do and say, and you can come out of the meditative state at any time.

Meditation is the next step up from dreaming. It's a way for you to start dreaming while actually awake. You do this by relaxing your mind into the alpha wave states associated with falling asleep or just waking up. During quiet and receptive meditation, one strives to find the gap between the constant chatter of thoughts. In this mental space you will find the point at which spirits can reach out to you and give you impressions, feelings, thoughts, and perceptions.

Before meditation, it is important to ground and center yourself. It can be emotionally and mentally exhausting to encounter a spirit during your waking life, so make sure that you start out feeling fresh. Meditation is difficult, there's no doubt about it. Creating a gap in between your thoughts is easier said than done. There are several tricks to try to snap your focus back onto your meditation, but be advised that none of them make the process easy. The only way to make meditation easier is through practice, as with any other physical or mental discipline.

As a beginner, it is especially important to reduce distractions before you meditate. That means turning off your phone and anything that beeps, locking yourself in a room where you won't be disturbed, and letting people know that you are busy. Set a timer. If you are new to meditation and have a naturally short attention span like I do, five minutes is not an unreasonable time for a first attempt. If you find it too challenging, or well within your ability, you can adjust the duration on the next attempt. The tricky part is that you'll need to give yourself enough time to settle into meditation and clear your mind as well as enough time to sit in that state and wait for a message from a spirit.

To clear your mind, focus on your breathing or your heartbeat. Focusing on your body in this way brings you into the present moment and away from thinking about what work you might need to do, or what you are going to eat after you meditate. Try square breathing: Breathing in for four heartbeats, holding your breath for four heartbeats, breathing out for four heartbeats, and then holding again for four heartbeats. Altering your breath in this way can be challenging at first, but it will slow your breathing rate and become more comfortable over the course of a few minutes.

To receive messages from a spirit, it helps to focus attention at your solar plexus. This is a psychic energy center, and it is believed that energy flowing from this area helps you sense spirits in your surroundings. By focusing your attention at your solar plexus, you theoretically expand your aura to detect spirits that share the room with you, enhancing communication. Whenever your attention wanders from your solar plexus due to thoughts, sounds, or sensations, bring your attention back to your solar plexus and continue.

A good way to maintain your focus and to welcome the spirit is to inwardly chant its name as a mantra when you meditate. You don't have to say the name of the spirit out loud. Inwardly say the name the same way that you might talk to yourself in your own mind when performing a complex activity. Whenever your mind wanders away from your focus point, snap it back in place by inwardly saying the name of the spirit. As a beginner, you might find that you have to refocus with each breath. As you become a more accomplished meditator, you'll find that you no longer need to do this as frequently.

As you learn to sit in the gap between thoughts, you will begin to receive messages from the spirit you have called. Every person experiences these messages in different ways. You might have the messages come to you as if they were your own thoughts, except that they feel strange to you, as if somebody else planted them there in your mind. You might see colors or shapes behind your closed eyelids. You may hear a voice in your head that sounds like your own or someone else's voice. This may sound similar to when you hear a song that has become stuck in your head. Some people might even perceive sounds and sights in the same way they see and hear things with their eyes and ears, but those experiences should end when the meditation ends.

Make sure to have paper and pen handy so you can write down or sketch your perceptions. Just like with dreams, things you experience during meditation may slip immediately from your short-term memory without sticking around. You don't have to disrupt your meditation by writing down things as they happen. It is okay to wait until the very end of your meditation session to write them all down, but make sure to record them before you get up to go about your day.

The hardest part about meditation is that it requires disciplined practice. I know it sounds easy to just sit there and do nothing while waiting for a spirit to communicate, but creating a gap of nothingness between your thoughts is easier said than done. A beginner probably won't sit down and have a successful communion with a spirit on his or her first try. It's disheartening, but don't give up.

The best part about using meditation is that it feels startlingly direct. Imagine speaking aloud to a deceased loved one and having the answer return to you as if you were having a conversation in life. You can access wisdom from spirits anytime without needing to dig out expensive or complicated tools. As a bonus, meditation is very good for you in and of itself. You'll receive the benefits of lower blood pressure and reduced stress, all while talking to a beloved spirit. These are all great reasons to recommend meditation as a way for your loved ones to talk to you after you're gone, as long as you don't think the learning curve would dissuade them from attempting meditation long enough for success.

Divination

In this context, divination refers to any system in which tools are used to understand agreed-upon meanings after specific procedures have been performed with the tools. There are countless forms of divination used in cultures the world over. Teaching every form of divination is of course beyond the scope of this book, but I'd like to explore in detail just a few that have tools which are especially easy to make or obtain, and those which might be particularly appropriate for a spirit you know. If you already happen to know some other form of divination, you are welcome to use it. If you're a complete beginner to divination, grab a friend who would like to try divination out for spirit communication, pick one of the methods below, and have fun with this crash course. I recommend choosing only one to try for each spirit communication session so you can get a real feel for it. As you go, think about which method you might want to use when you are a spirit, and try to gain the sense of perspective from the other side.

Yes/No Stone

Let's start with the simplest divination technique available. Go find a stone outside. It should be a relatively flat stone that fits into the palm of your hand so you can flip it like a coin and allow it to fall on one side in your hand or on the ground. You'll also need an opaque bag, such as a velvet drawstring bag, and some paint or a pen. Write "yes" on one side of the stone and "no" on the other. To use the stone during spirit communication, you can shake the bag and fish out the stone, taking the first answer you see, or you can flip the stone. Obviously, this divination technique is quite limited, but it is certainly clear and useful for those who feel intimidated by divination, or for those who like the convenience of flipping a coin.

Casting Bones, Runes, or Ogham

Casting bones is an appropriate way to contact spirits, and it certainly has a spooky feel to it. Many cultures have used bone casting in some form or another. To cast bones, you'll first need to collect some clean and dry bones. I recommend chicken bones. I'm a vegetarian, so I enlist the help of my carnivore husband to save bones for spiritual activities from time to time. I've also collected old and dry cattle bones in the desert and from a farm. Collect bones that are all similar in size; at least nine of them. When they are all clean and dry, you can keep them in a small bag and shake the bag out onto a surface to interpret their positions.

You might want to draw a circle or a line on a surface or a piece of paper before scattering bones, and there are several ways they can be read. Drawing a circle limits the interpretation only to those bones which fall inside it. Drawing a line shows the bones below the line as depicting the past, the life of the person before he or she became a spirit. Above the line represents the future, and bone arrangements that fall touching the line represent the present.

One way to look at bones is to examine the formations. For example, if a group of bones fall and form a square, it represents stability. Arrows up can represent ascension or advancement, while arrows down represent hardship and challenge. Arrows to the right represent the future; to the left, the past. A triangle can represent the instability associated with growth. Use your imagination to see other shapes and decide upon an interpretation. If you draw a circle and only interpret some of the bones, you can find meaning by counting the number of bones that fall inside the circle. For example:

1. Assertiveness, aggression; loneliness; individuality; a spirit feeling abandoned by loved ones

2. Love, a meeting of minds; first sight of something or someone new; a spirit with love for you

3. Creativity, growth; a new child, a spirit who is part of your family

4. Stability, the home; entrapment; a spirit who offers protection or lives in your house

5. Play; challenge, difficulty, instability, push and pull, argument; a spirit with unresolved conflict

6. Profit; learning, improvement through knowledge and study; a spirit with a lesson to teach

7. Mystery, spirituality; femininity; deception; a spirit with a message about divinity or afterlife

8. Success, financial stability, triumph; growth; a spirit who offers support for your material goals

9. Joy; achieving goals; luck; good fortune brought by a spirit watching over you

It takes practice to combine the number of bones with the storyline the formations create, but when you do, it can provide a message for you from the spirit. You can combine a circle and a line drawn on the throwing surface to increase complexity, as well as adding other indicators drawn on the throwing surface. You can see how adding a yes/no stone to the bone throwing mix would also increase the amount of information transmitted.

There are other casting (throwing) arts that may be of interest to you if bones are right up your alley. Casting bones is a spooky, fun way to contact spirits and can really get you into the feel of working with death in a positive way. Of course, the downside is that the messages are often pretty general.

Runes—Runes are a set of numerous stones with signs written on each one. Each sign has a meaning ascribed to it. The way that the stones fall (in addition to their face meaning) can be read to transmit a message. Norse and Germanic runes are a popular form of divination today, so if your ancestors come from those regions, you may find runes to be an especially appropriate way to contact those ancestral spirits.

Ogham—Characters written on sticks can be used instead of bones or stones. Ogham ("OH-wum") is a Celtic system that may appeal to spirits of Celtic ancestral origin. Again, the symbols on the ogham sticks can be interpreted along with the sticks' positions.

Dowsing

Dowsing is a name given to the practice where a person uses an object that can move or swing freely to receive a spirit message given by pointing a direction. Dowsing can be done easily with tools that can be made by hand. You can extend your dowsing by creating a dowsing board. Get a piece of paper and draw letters, numbers, or other messages that can be indicated using a dowsing object. Dowsing is exciting because it feels direct, like you're allowing the spirit to dictate its movement. Don't worry if it is obviously your hand controlling the dowsing tool. Dowsing can also be a way to extend your own intuition into a more clear expression. Keep in mind that this method does take some practice and concentration—two things that might be in short supply for the recently bereaved. Here are four different methods of dowsing you can use with materials found around the house.

Dowsing stick—A dowsing stick was traditionally used to find water. The branch is Y-shaped, and you can find one outdoors or make one yourself. The user holds the stick by the two shorter ends and, the tip of the stick will seem to waver and indicate a direction of its own accord. Go with the movement and follow it. A dowsing stick can help a spirit guide you to a sacred space, a lost item, or a spot on a map or dowsing board.

Dowsing rods—You can make dowsing rods from lengths of stiff copper wire. A simple wire coat hanger can be used in a pinch. Cut the wire into two pieces, each about the length of your arm, and then bend them into an L-shape. Hold one dowsing rod in each hand by the short end of the L and allow the long ends to swing freely. When extended in front of you, hold them loosely, so that they are allowed to point in a direction or cross over each other. As you walk, a spirit can indicate that you should stop walking by allowing the dowsing rods to cross. Dowsing rods can be used in the same way as a dowsing stick, but they move more freely.

Pendulum—A pendulum is a plumb bob hanging from a chain or string. You can make your own pendulum using a ring and a length of string or a necklace chain. Of course, this tool may work better for you if the jewelry came from the deceased person in question. To use the pendulum, dangle it from its lead between your thumb and index finger, then loop the string or chain over your pinkie finger so that the pendulum or ring swings freely. Ask the pendulum to show you what "yes" looks like. It will most likely either swing back and forth or begin to swing in circle, counter-clockwise or clockwise. That is your indicator for the answer "yes" from a spirit. Ask the pendulum what "no" looks like, and note the answer. Now you can use the pendulum the way you use other dowsing tools as well as how you might use a yes/no stone. The pendulum is a more precise indicator on dowsing boards since it is small and easy to wield.

Body dowsing—You can dowse for "yes" or "no" answers without any tools at all by just using your body, although this does take a degree of balance and should not be attempted if you have issues with standing or with mobility. Stand with your feet together, close your eyes, and ask to be shown what "yes" looks like. You may feel your body tipping back and forth, left or right, or wobbling in a circle clockwise or counterclockwise. Next, ask what "no" looks like and note the response from your body. Now you can ask simple questions and get simple answers with no tools at all.

Dowsing can actually feel like a very exciting experience of speaking with spirits, because it can sometimes feel like your body is being literally led by some external spirit force, while still allowing you to be in control of what happens. One spiritual teacher of mine, (I'll call him Dave) taught me copper rod dowsing in an especially fine lesson. A group of friends and I had come to his house to learn dowsing, and, lucky for us, his house happened to be very old and very haunted. Dave enjoyed telling us stories about a spirit who lived there, and even boasted that he had a human jaw bone he believed belonged to the spirit's body in life.

He brought out a roll of copper wire and cut it into proper lengths so we could experience copper wire dowsing. Each of us bent the copper wire into large L shapes, and soon we were all standing up, walking around and giggling as our wire shapes pointed all over the house. Some people were asking for the dowsing rods to find water, and were tracing the water piping in the walls. Suddenly, one of my friends realized that she had forgotten where she had put her mobile phone. Perhaps it was in the other room. Dave stopped me when I offered to call her phone with my own. "Let my house spirit show us," he suggested. He then walked to the closest wall and intoned, "Spirit, please show us where the missing phone lies!" He then rapped on the wall three times with his knuckles.

We waited quietly. All at once, everyone who was standing with their dowsing rods in hand, saw them all swing around, and point in unison toward the room in which we had been using the wire cutters. Silence fell over us all, and I heard three slow knocks come from that direction, as if the spirit were banging from somewhere inside the walls. Stunned, we drifted into the other room and, after scanning the area, found that the phone was indeed lying beneath a chair in that room. It was an exciting shared experience with my friends, and it felt as if we had been transported back to the days when Spiritualism was something practiced in living rooms everywhere.

Bibliomancy

Bibliomancy is the art of flipping open a book at random to receive a message from spirit by pointing to a random word or phrase and seeking meaning. Bibliomancy works best with books that are either brand new or evenly worn so faults in the spine won't result in the book falling open to the same well-worn pages each time. Some perform bibliomancy by selecting a random number instead of physically flipping the pages. You can choose any book for bibliomancy, but most practitioners choose prayer books or scripture such as the Bible for Christians, the Odù Ifá for Yoruba people, or the *Bhagavad Gita* or other Vedic scriptures for Hindus.

To perform bibliomancy, simply flip the book open at random and point to a page with your eyes closed. Open your eyes and interpret by the letter, word, phrase, sentence, or the entire page. Continue the process until you build an entire meaningful message from the spirit. Bibliomancy can be especially helpful if you choose a book your ancestor had a special relationship with in life.

To make your own bibliomancy resource using an alphabet to spell out words, get twenty-six pieces of paper and write one letter of the alphabet on each page. Sticky notes work great for this, but you can also punch a hole and use a locking ring to hold sheets together and allow yourself to mix up the letters if needed (to prevent yourself from purposefully choosing letters based on their position in the alphabet). Using alphabetic bibliomancy is especially helpful if you are trying to identify a spirit's name. Flip through the lettered pages at random while speaking with the spirit. You can also add numbers. Only flip through the letters if you are asking a question that can be answered verbally, and flip through the numbers if you are asking a question that has to do with dates, ages, or other numerical answers. The letters "Y" and "N" can also be indicators for yes and no.

My mother had a powerful bibliomancy experience while she was on a spiritual pilgrimage to Israel, and this experience actually changed her faith tradition. Though she had always been a spiritual person and believed in both God and magic, she was not committed to worship according to any one faith. At least not until the day she traveled to Haifa to visit the shrine of the Baha'i messianic figure, Bahá'u'lláh. While at the grave site, she could feel the presence of his spirit as a sense of power or thickness in the air that urged her to be reverent. She bowed down at the threshold of the room where his remains were interred. There, she began to pray for some time. Soon she felt the presence of God, as well, manifesting as a light behind her closed eyelids. She rose up to a kneeling position and asked if there were any messages for her from spirit. Clutched in her hands was a brand-new Baha'i prayer book. She flipped through the onionskin pages and the book fell open to a random passage that spoke to her. It was a prayer that happened to be directed to the faithful in her adopted country. Her emotional state quickly caused tears to obscure most of the words as she continued turning over the pages. The only terms she could make out were those that expounded on the theme of servitude or service. She took all this as a message from spirit to join and serve her Baha'i community at home, and she began to do so as soon as she returned from her pilgrimage.

Tea Leaf Reading

Tea leaf reading is one of my favorite forms of scrying. Scrying is the act of looking for shapes or symbols within a tool, in this case within the random arrangements of tea leaves. More advanced than looking at an arrangement of bones or stones, the leaves can clump together to make shapes that look more like pictures. The reason tea leaf reading is so wonderful for spirit communication is because it involves the wonderful ritual of taking tea. Imagine being able to have a cup of tea with a loved one, even after they have gone. Tea leaf reading provides quiet contemplation that can be therapeutic and rewarding. Here is how to have a cup of tea with a deceased loved one.

Step 1) Procure a teacup with a rounded bottom and a saucer. Get yourself some loose leaf tea. The smaller the leaves the better when they are wet. Otherwise you'll just be looking at a giant blob. Heat your water and apply it directly to the tea leaves in the cup without use of a strainer or other cage for the tea leaves.

Step 2) Wait for your tea to cool and sit in contemplation as you sip it. Ground yourself. The hardest part is drinking your tea without inadvertently sucking up the leaves. You may wish to use a strainer straw at this point to allow the tea leaves to continue to float freely as you drink. Leave only a tiny bit of water in the bottom. Too much water and your saucer will overflow when you overturn your cup.

Step 3) Swirl the cup three times clockwise and then quickly turn it upside down onto the saucer. Flip the cup back over. You should see small clumps of tea leaves at the bottom and on the sides of the inside of the cup. These are what you will be interpreting in the next step.

Step 4) The tea leaves in the bottom of the cup represent the past and the present, while those further up on the sides represent the future, in progression. Now, you can take a look at the shapes of the leaves and interpret them with respect to the timing. Look at them the way that you would look at clouds in the sky. Do any of them look like animals? Letters? Little people performing actions? Use your imagination to tell a story.

Step 5) Make sketches and notes about what you see in your teacup. Some of the pictures may seem like a riddle in the moment, but their meaning may become clearer after you've had some time to think about them. The best part about tea leaf reading is that you can show others your teacup as well, and ask what they see. Sometimes others may be able to hit the nail on the head with a tea leaf reading that you find confusing.

I've had countless spirit experiences alone and with others when performing tea leaf readings. One I can remember off the top of my head was when I was reading tea leaves at an event for a local adoption organization. The organization had hired me to read tea leaves at a charity fundraiser dinner. It delighted me to be paid to sit in a luxury hotel where my every wish was accommodated. I was given a lovely foyer for reading, and a beautiful oak table with china cups were also provided. All I had to bring was the loose leaf tea.

The people at the benefit were all allowed unlimited free readings, since the organization was paying my hourly rate. Many people chose to ask questions about ancestor spirits since, as this was an adoption organization after all, many there were about to become parents for the first time and were eager to consult with deceased parents and grandparents about their exciting new stage in life. One woman asked if she could speak with her grandmother through the tea leaf reading, and I told her she was welcome to try. She sat with me quietly as she sipped her tea.

When the tea leaves were ready to be read, she looked at the wet leaves in her cup with deep interest. "I see a flag," she said. "What does that mean?" I looked in her cup to confirm the presence of the flag and saw a boat next to it. I told her that a flag typically means a nation, and that the boat next to the flag made me think that it was encouraging travel to another country across the water. The woman was excited and told me that she was planning a trip overseas to her grandmother's country of origin to visit a child she was planning to adopt from an orphanage. She took her tea leaf reading as a sign that her grandmother approved. She was so touched by the process that she planned to start doing tea leave readings herself and to have tea with her grandmother on a regular basis.

Scrying in Water

I love water scrying because it feels so ancient. Water was humanity's first mirror, and when I gaze into water meditatively, I feel connected somehow to all who have gone before me, who may also have looked to the surface of still waters in moments of solitude. Water scrying can feel different, however. During one session, it might look like a real mirror, in which I can see spirits as people standing behind my own reflection, as if they were in the same room and I could see them if I turned around. Another time, my experience might be much more subtle, with the light playing on the water simply inspiring my eyes to imagine symbols that are meaningful to me, such as a heart shape or the first letter of a name.

Scrying in water can be considerably more difficult than tea leaf reading, because it involves deeper concentration. Some people won't literally see images in the water to interpret. However, I include water scrying for two reasons. First, water scrying is a traditional resource in séances. Second, water is easily available just about anywhere. So, if you invest the time required to develop water scrying skill, you'll be able to whip out a bowl of water and talk with spirits anywhere and any time.

Step 1) You'll first need a bowl of water. Select either a black bowl or a highly reflective silver bowl. Either of these bowls can produce a concave lens effect that helps trick your eyes into soft focus, which is easier for meditation and scrying. Make sure your bowl doesn't have any decorations around the rim, because that can be distracting.

Step 2) Once you fill your bowl with water, you might want to add a few drops of oil, as is traditional for séances. Some also choose to add a small crystal, such as a piece of quartz, to the bowl of water.

Step 3) Ground yourself. Allow yourself to meditate with your eyes closed for a bit before scrying in the bowl of water. You'll need to rid yourself of external distractions so that you can pay attention to perceptions from the spirit which originate from within you.

Step 4) Open your eyes and gaze into the bowl with a soft focus for a period of time. Meditate with your eyes open. At this point, some might perceive messages in the same way as they do with their usual meditative spirit communication. However, the bowl of water may act as a visual aid for you to see pictures in your mind's eye. Some people may even perceive imagery in the bowl of water itself, almost as if it were a television screen, but don't be discouraged if that's not your experience right away. It may take time for you to develop skills and talents.

Step 5) Write down any feelings or perceptions you
had while gazing into the bowl of water. Since you
were deep in meditation, these thoughts may easily
be forgotten once you are finished. It is important
for you to write your notes down quickly when you
are done.

Spirit Board or Talking Board

A talking board, also called a spirit board, is a board of
letters and numbers as well as "yes," "no," and sometimes
other symbols, too. Just like a dowsing board, these messages are indicated with a spirit through use of a tool, which
for a talking board or spirit board is called a "planchette."
A planchette is most often a lens mounted on top of an
apparatus that can glide freely across the board's surface
when pushed or pulled just a single finger. A Ouija Board
is a specific brand of talking board licensed by Hasbro as
of this book's writing. Ouija Boards are made of cardboard
and plastic, but they can still be used to talk with spirits.

In fact, as mentioned earlier, you can make your own
talking board that works just as well as ones mass produced in factories. Any sheet of paper and pen will do.
I will keep calling it a talking board, even if what you've
made is more like a talking sheet of paper. Select a glass
to use as your planchette. You may need to try a few different glasses to see which slides most easily on the piece
of paper. Short glasses are best as they are more difficult
to tip over. After you have chosen your glass, write down
the letters of the alphabet such that they are about the

size of the mouth of the glass to be clearly indicated. Letters indicated with a shot glass, therefore, would be much smaller than those indicated by a wine glass or beer stein. Write down the numbers zero through nine and the answers "yes" and "no" as well. It doesn't matter where these answers are located on the piece of paper.

Whatever you chose to make your talking board with, the method is always the same. Place your fingers gently on the planchette while it rests in the center of the board. It works best when one or two fingers from each hand on the planchette is used so that your wrists don't rest too heavily upon the planchette, weighing it down. More information on using a talking board in a group setting is included in the section on séances.

As with the pendulum, the planchette should seem to move on its own, even if it is your own hand motions guiding it. Some users even purposely push the planchette around too quickly to control its movements, trusting in the spirits to guide one's hands to a coherent message. Such a technique can be very useful if you are trying to transmit a very long message from an especially eager spirit. In fact, the spirit board has been used to channel several published novels, and it is my belief that they must have used this faster method. A slower use of the board, however, may engender a deeper feeling of connection and reverence. You can try resting your hands on the planchette without purposefully moving it but without holding it down if it feels like it is beginning to move. Cultivate your meditation skills for this method, as it may take five minutes of still-ness before you notice anything happening.

As with everything else, make sure to write down the messages you receive through a talking board. In particular, talking boards lend themselves well to writing messages down. If the planchette is moving quickly, the volume of words that may come through will be too much to remem-ber. If the planchette is moving slowly, you might be work-ing in a trance state that makes you forget what was com-municated as soon as the session is finished. Don't let those important messages turn into vague stories of "something" strange happening—write things down.

I could write an entire book on the experiences with spirits I've had while using a spirit board, and in fact, I have. I've seen a daughter cry to see the words of her mother. I've seen a lover collapse in relief at seeing a sign that her old flame could send word from beyond the grave. Through the spirit board I've enjoyed being able to meet spirits I have never known during their lifetimes. The lettering method of the spirit board makes spirit communication as simple as reading a book, and I've been blessed to meet new spirits who have regaled me with their stories.

Other Forms of Divination

There are so many beautiful forms of divination the world over that it is impossible to include them all here. Now that I have gone over in depth the forms that can be easily learned with equipment found around anyone's home, I'd like to go over some other popular modes of divination and why they might be used instead. You don't have to practice all of these methods with your loved ones before you die, but if one of them speaks to you or to your next of kin in particular, it is worth investigating.

Crystal Ball Reading—A crystal ball has traditionally been a tool for séances, replaced with a bowl of water with drops of oil when a quartz sphere is not available. Any size quartz crystal ball will do for spirit communication, as long as it is true crystal and not glass. The way that you can tell the difference is that a glass sphere is usually clear, while a crystal ball has tiny flaws that look like shiny flakes or strands. It is in those imperfections that you will look for shapes, just as in tea leaf reading. The best thing about crystal ball reading is that you can interpret the colors in the shapes as well as the shapes themselves. The most challenging thing is that you can easily lose sight of the shapes you are studying if you turn the crystal, and it is nearly impossible to show somebody what you are looking at, since a slight change in the angle of viewing can make the shapes look very different. Thus, no two crystal ball scrying sessions are alike, even with the same crystal ball.

When performing spirit communication for other people (such as during a séance), the crystal ball tends to be my go-to tool. To me, it feels less limited than tarot cards and yet still gives me a powerful tool so I don't have to feel the pressure of trying to generate a vision of a spirit with nothing else but my closed eyes. When I use a crystal ball, I usually describe people as clearly as I can from the images of them I see in the flecks within the sphere. I remember at one point I saw a spirit when I was reading for a woman who had not asked for a spirit reading at all. She had asked for an appointment with me to ask about her business, but when I described a man I saw in the crystal, wondering if it might be a business partner, she said that it was her late husband who had perished in a car accident. Apparently, I had even correctly described the outfit he was wearing when he died. She had originally started the business with her husband, and was delighted to be able to get some business advice from his spirit.

Ifá—This Yoruba method of divination makes use of shells that are casted as lots. Each arrangement of shells corresponds to advice from a system of texts called the *Odu*. Though this system requires careful study for correct interpretation, it can be worth pursuing, especially for those communicating with Yoruba ancestors.

I Ching—This Chinese system of divination interprets hexagrams and trigrams that correspond to the layout of coins or, traditionally, yarrow sticks that are cast as lots. Each resulting hexagram or trigram has an agreed-upon meaning. This complex divination has a learning curve but can be worth it, especially for those reaching out to Chinese ancestors.

Palmistry—Palmistry may seem a silly way to communicate with spirits if you think your palms never change, but they do. Small colored dots or blotches can appear on your hands minute to minute, and over the weeks or months even the lines and other major hand features can change. If you perform spirit communication infrequently, palmistry can be a good way to link yourself to your ancestry, especially your parents since it was they who made those hands in the first place. There are specific parts of your palms that refer to specific relatives, as well, so checking your hands are a good way to know who is talking when you are communicating with a spirit. Look on both your hands carefully for the following, keeping in mind that some of these marks may appear or disappear depending on what message a spirit has for you.

For example, my grandmother was always a pretty spirited lady in my memory, and she never let a sense of propriety stop her from feeling angry. If I roll over in bed in the morning and spot a red dot appearing in my lower, right palm, near the percussive side (the side you'd use to make a karate chop), I know that there will be some people making me angry that day, and that I'd better watch my tongue. I seem to have inherited her fearsome temper, and she knows how to warn me about it!

Mom—A red or pink line on the lunar mount on the percussive side of your hand.

Dad—A line or branch from your destiny line on your mount of Saturn under your ring finger.

Kids—Lines on your Mercury mount, underneath your pinkie finger, rising or descending perpendicular to relationship lines that lie horizontally from the percussive edge of your palm.

Sister—Markings found on the mount of Pluto at the base of your palm on the inside of the lunar mount (found on the lower percussive edge of your palm). Your sisters, or spiritual sisters, can be shown as any lines or dots.

Brother—Markings found on the mount of Pluto at the base of your palm on the inside of your mount of Venus (found at the base of your thumb).

Grandma—Markings found within the lunar mount at the lower percussive edge of your palm.

Grandpa—Markings found at the lower end of your
destiny line (rising line to your middle finger).
They can also appear as a branch on your mount
of Saturn from that same line.

Cousin—Markings found above your lunar mount,
at the lower percussive edge of your palm.

Wife—Either a cross on your mount of Apollo under
your ring finger or a horizontal line under your
pinkie finger coming from the percussive edge
of your hand, or both.

Husband—Same as the signs for a wife above, or can
also be a rising line from your lunar mount (on the
lower percussive edge of your hand) to either your
middle finger or ring finger.

Lover—A serious lover whom you simply may not
have included in your family in any way can be
shown as an Apollo cross in your hand low under
your ring finger. This person may also be found as
a mark along the heart line, especially one on the
mount of Jupiter under your pointer finger.

The hardest part about divination is that every form
takes some preparation to procure the tools or learn the
required skills. If you do spirit communication only a few
times a year, you might lose it in between sessions. And
even if you really love a specific form of divination, you
might find out that your loved ones hate it and are not

likely to want to use it to contact *your* spirit later on. That's why it is so important to practice divination with your loved ones while you are still alive; everyone involved can get a feel for what it's like.

The best part about divination is that the messages that come through can be very clear—clear enough to write a book of quotes from your loved one or for you to be quoted from beyond the grave. Many forms of divination are so straightforward that you don't need to be particularly intuitive or spiritual to use them. If loved ones want to talk to you and aren't keen on becoming fanatical mystics, they can always find a method of divination that feels as simple as reading a book.

Séances

Séances are a spirit communication session that includes more than one living person in the process. Typically, a séance has one master of ceremonies called the medium, and one or more guests who listen to the spirit communication through the medium or simply offer their energy and support to the cause. However, séances can include more than one medium; every living participant in the séance can act as a medium as well. A séance is a great way to include family members or loved ones who might otherwise feel overwhelmed with the idea of learning a whole new skill set and reaching outside their comfort zones to explore belief systems.

For many, selecting a designated medium may be a good precaution or encouragement for spirit communication. If you have one family member who is very open to spirit communication and others who are not, designating him or her as a medium can ensure that séances will be held in which your other family members will be welcome.

You may also want to designate a medium if you have the opposite problem—many people who might want to step into that role, some more productively than others. Designating one medium can keep people from bickering or ensure that only a person who has your best wishes in mind can communicate with you in spirit directly. Choosing a medium may actually be best if you want your spirit communication to be limited to one generation. Maybe you want to be there for your loved ones for the rest of their lives but then left in peace afterwards. In that case, once your designated medium comes to join you in the afterlife, your spirit communication is ended as well.

You can designate a medium for séances after your death. In life, you can practice with that medium by sharing the medium duties during the séance while learning together. A séance can be practiced through simple meditation or with any form of divination, but traditionally it has been done with a bowl of water with a few drops of oil added, a crystal ball, or a spirit board/talking board. It is best to choose only one during a single session so that all participants can understand what is going on and feel comfortable with the methods used. Before starting, make sure you're familiar with at least one of those techniques.

Steps for performing a séance

Step 1) Gather your materials. You'll need a preferably round table with enough chairs for all participants. Decide whether you are going to go without any form of divination and simply meditate, or whether you want to use a traditional divination tool such as a crystal ball, bowl of water and oil, or spirit board/talking board.

Step 2) Decide who will be present at the séance. It is best to call only one spirit for a séance, so decide whom you might want to speak with. Invite family and friends, based on who wishes to communicate with the spirit in question. Think of all the family and mutual friends who might be interested and invite them all; you may be surprised at who shows up. You can invite people to bring photos of the deceased or mementos, but they're not necessary for the séance to work.

Step 3) Explain any divination system that will be used as well as the preparation for spirit communication to those who may not be familiar with these practices. Agree ahead of time who wants to be mediums and what questions are appropriate to ask the spirit during the séance. Everybody should feel comfortable

with what will be going on, so don't change the
séance in the middle unless everybody agrees.

Step 4) Everyone should seat themselves at the table
with the divination system (if any) placed in the
middle of the table. Explain and guide grounding.
At the beginning, everyone should put both palms
flat on the table and then push hands forward so that
everyone's pinkie fingers are touching. That way, you
are all linked in the process, but if one person becomes
uncomfortable, it is easy to simply slide one's hands
back off the table and stop personally participating. If
using a spirit board or talking board, everyone starts
the séance with hands on the table, but then breaks
the connection to reconnect on the planchette.

Step 5) Spirit communication should take place
according to the method of choice. Afterwards, any
messages should be written down, no matter how
many witnesses are present; some people remember
things differently than others afterward.

Step 6) Make sure to guide and direct grounding again
for all present. Debrief to see how everybody is
feeling. A séance can evoke some pretty intense
emotions. It is best to ask how everyone is feeling
right away so that there aren't any hard feelings
between any of you later on if somebody feels
uncomfortable. Debriefing will also allow you to
gauge who might want to come to another séance.

The hardest part about séances is teaching everybody how to participate, especially if somebody else wants to be the medium. It is good news if somebody wants to learn how to be a medium, because it means he or she might act as a medium after your death. However, it may require more preparation. Take a look at the "Things to Consider" questions at the end of this chapter for some ideas about how to prepare other people to be mediums.

The best part about séances is the shared experience that can make family and friendship bonds closer. It is amazing when everyone participating in a séance experiences the same message at the same time. Group séances can feel incredibly validating, because corroboration makes the experience feel more real. A regular practice of séances can help you and your loved ones remove all doubt that there is life after death.

Spirit Communication in Eight Simple Steps: The Chauran Method

Hopefully this whirlwind crash-course on spirit communication will leave you feeling inspired and excited to get started. I've provided you with all of the components of spirit communication with lots of opportunities for customization. You may have observed that there are many different ways to do all of the exercises you've learned in this chapter, so it may seem challenging for a beginner to understand how to put everything into a coherent whole. I'd like to provide a simplified example for a solitary spirit communication session using my own preferences. Needless to say, you'll just have to wait until I'm gone to summon my particular spirit!

Step 1) Gather your supplies. Suggested divination tool: A pre-fab spirit board or a handmade talking board. Optional offerings: white snapdragons, a cup of black tea, frankincense incense.

Step 2) Optionally, wait for the best time. Ideal times are at the end of October, the beginning of May, or during a full moon, but any time can be used if there is a true need or desire.

Step 3) Prepare the space. Take yourself to any doorway, set up your offerings, and prepare for spirit communication thusly:

    a. Ground and center yourself. Check in with your body and feelings. Visualize pushing any excess energy out through your feet harmlessly into the earth. Draw fresh, calming, rejuvenating energy back up from the earth into your body. Assess how you feel again before proceeding.

    b. Turn counterclockwise three times within the doorway while visualizing all negativity leaving to cleanse the space.

    c. Cense the space around you with frankincense, again in a circle to surround you three times.

You can visualize a boundary being drawn to protect you and to contain the spirit energy during your session.

d. (Optional) Pray something like:

> I invoke [God(s)/Goddess(es)/Spirit/ Universe/my higher self/etc.].
>
> You who are the provender of all spirits and the source of all communion.
>
> Thank you for aiding spirit communication and protecting me now.
>
> With harm to none, and for the highest good of all. So may it be.
>
> In return, I offer you [Love, willingness to spread the communicated message, etc.]
>
> Blessed be.

Step 4) Invoke using Alexandra Chauran's invocation chant.

> Alexandra, word doctor, witch:
> Close my eyes and count to three.
> Conjure spirit where I sit
> that magic and a future see.
> Blessed be.

Step 5) If you decided to use a talking board or spirit board, now is the time. Otherwise, sit in meditation to receive messages. Thank the spirit when you are done.

Step 6) Write down any messages that come through.

Step 7) After spirit communication, cense the area again to cleanse the space. You might visualize the energy disappearing, fading, being destroyed or withdrawn.

Step 8) Ground yourself, and leave the offerings outdoors.

Things to Consider

1. Choose a form of divination and learn how to use it to read for spirit communications.

2. Prepare to teach another person a form of divination, even if it is something as simple as a yes/no stone. Think about how you will explain what divination means to you and how to use it for spirit communication.

3. When is the best time for you to perform spirit communication? Think about how you can fit it into your life and your busy schedule. How can you build regular spirit communication into your calendar right now?

4. Write out a step-by-step plan for communicating with your spirit, as I did with my example in this chapter. Consider showing it to somebody else to see if it makes sense. Edit it if they have questions to make sure it is clear.

5. Plan a séance! Who will you invite? What is the best day and time? How do you think the people you know will react? What can you do to make the experience both comfortable and fun?

CHAPTER THREE

Afterlife Beliefs
and Faith Development

Today, while I was driving my three-year-old to preschool on this chilly October morning, she piped up from the back seat: "When it was dark, there was a woman in my room."

"Oh?" I asked with calm interest, "was she a nice woman?"

"Yes," Eris replied. "She laid down next to me in my bed, but it didn't tickle because I couldn't feel her. She was my great-grandmother."

"What was her name?" I asked, wondering whether it was my Grandma Bessie or somebody from my husband's side of the family.

Eris was startled by this question. "Oh, I don't know! But why was the woman there?"

I paused before asking. "Why do you think?"

My daughter rambled in true preschooler fashion. "Because I think that I am going to be a mother someday. And she was a grandmother…And a great-grandmother. She said I had a nice haircut! But why do you think the woman was in my room?"

I smiled and chuckled at the compliment about her haircut. "Eris, I believe that spirits or ghosts can come to help us. Maybe she wanted to be your friend and to keep you safe, or maybe she wanted to tell you a story. You can ask her next time, if you like."

The purpose of this chapter is to help you determine your own beliefs and faith. We are doing this for two reasons. Firstly, a coherent belief system is helpful when navigating spirit communication, as it helps you direct your conversation and methods. Secondly, spirit communication can help you find a strong faith within yourself so you don't have to fear death during life. Building a belief system into your everyday life from the understandings you gain through spirit communication is one of its major benefits.

The whole point of all of these exercises is to grow your faith and confidence during your lifetime so you no longer have to fear death's eventual arrival. Through your active communication with spirits while you're still alive, you'll be able to catch a glimpse of what your spirit existence will be like. Through real experiences, you'll be able to begin piecing together a solid understanding of your own belief system. Perhaps the spirits you summon will tell you directly. Or, you might be able to piece together clues from the impressions you get after many séances or spirit communication sessions.

What Happens After Death?

One of my first spirit communication experiences as a child frightened me, and not because the spirit was mean or scary. When I contacted the spirit through a spirit board, she simply kept telling me how lonely she was, and how happy she was that I had contacted her. At first, I took this to mean that she was completely alone after death, trapped in some kind of place where nobody ever spoke with her. I remember lying awake at night as a teen, frightened that it would be my fate to forever be silent and hoping somebody would talk to me. As an adult, I have had many more spirit communications that have contradicted that belief. Dead friends have told me that they've run into talkative relatives of mine in the afterlife they never knew in the lifetime we shared together. My mother and I have even spoken about interactions my father had with other spirits after death. During one meditative session with him, he tried to explain.

It was Halloween night and I had entered simple meditation while in a sacred circle space to talk to my dad, as I do every Halloween. In this particular session, it felt like my body rose up and flew out a door in the corner of the room, even though I was quite positive that my body was actually still seated on the floor. When I met with my dad, it was in an unearthly blackness, as if we had no need for the artifices of a visual spiritual landscape. It had been years since he died, so I spoke like we were catching up after a vacation, rather than as a grieving daughter. With curiosity, I asked him what he did much of the day. He told me that he had seen some of my proud moments in life and that he had met my children, which brought me joy. But he also said that he kept busy in the world that he occupied as well. When I asked him to explain it to me, he said that there was no real earthly equivalent, but that I could think of his role as similar to the leadership role he assumed at a housing organization while he lived. I was satisfied with his answer at the time. I also asked him what the moment of death was like and he said that it wasn't scary for him.

A few months before my dad died, his beloved cat had died peacefully. He had said that he would like to go just like that, and my guess is that he did.

We all wonder what happens after death, for the awareness of mortality is one of the blessings and curses of being human. Across cultures and religions are a few belief themes that return again and again, and some of them may reflect the truth. At the very least, belief in them is an essential part of the human experience. As you read through some of these examples, assess how you feel about them. You may have an immediate emotional reaction. Some may seem to have face value. Some may sound scary or soothing. Later, as you gain experience with spirit communication, I'd like you to try reading through them again to see which ones match up with the evidence you have received through your direct experiences with, and messages from, spirits.

Peace

Imagine a death in which nothing happens at all. Eternal peace and rest are the only function of death, so the toils—and joys—of life are completely gone. For some people, the idea of losing all personality and the memories of a lifetime sounds terrifying. For others, it is a good thing. For example, many Christians believe that dead people are in a deep and dreamless slumber, waiting for the return of the messiah. Many Buddhists and Hindus actually strive for this endless peace, believing that the cycle of life and death is tiring, and that reincarnation is something one needs to eventually escape.

The existence of peace after death does not necessarily exclude spirit communication. Some believe that a part of the soul rests while another part can communicate. Or, there could be a difference in the way the living and the dead experience time. What may be a brief moment of spirit communication before eternal rest may be an entire human lifetime or generations of human life. There are those who believe spirits exist in a peaceful slumber until they are summoned, and that they can return to that peace between sessions.

Reincarnation

Reincarnation is the idea that after a person dies, at some point his or her soul is recycled into living existence either in a human, animal, or some other form of life. The point of reincarnation varies in the teachings of different religions. For some Buddhists and Hindus, we may be learning lessons to escape the cycle of death and rebirth collectively or as individuals. For some NeoPagans, although individuals are learning lessons, there is no final goal except for continued joy each time one returns to earth and reunites with loved ones in different forms. Life here on earth is wonderful because only here do we have a perfect union of mind, body, and spirit, easily within the grasp of people who choose to be born here. New Age practitioners introduced the idea to the mainstream that some past lives can be remembered, although other faith traditions maintain that the lives are forgotten each time.

An Afterlife in Heaven, Summerland, or Nirvana

Many religions visualize the afterlife as a paradise. For many Christians, heaven is a place where there is no suffering, and where the presence of God is very close. In heaven, all loved ones are reunited. For the Baha'i, the afterlife represents an evolution of existence. Though it cannot be fathomed, it contains joys that cannot be experienced here on earth.

For Wiccans, the concept of the Summerland evokes feelings of the joys of the warm season, and it is often thought to be a place of rest and rejuvenation before rebirth. Other Neo-Pagans anticipate a temporary or permanent paradise in Valhalla or Avalon, believing that souls sail across the mythical waters of emotion and grief to rest there.

Since the concept of paradise differs from person to person, some don't think of the heavenly afterlife as a pain-free version of life here on earth. For those who want to escape the cycle of life, heaven is simply freedom from desire, or Nirvana, which can even be achieved during life. During death, such freedom would manifest as union with God or eternal peace.

I would be remiss to talk about an afterlife of paradise without addressing the inverse, which some faith traditions call hell, the underworld, or disconnection from God. Not all religions claim there is a place of disconnection from God or suffering to which one can go after death; however, the fear is valid for many people. One reason to practice spirit communication is to move past the fear of a negative experience in the afterlife by talking with spirits who have already passed. If spirits who reach you have escaped the fate you fear, then certainly you can as well.

Ghosts

Most people who undertake spirit communication believe in ghosts or manifestations of spirits that exist right here on earth. Ghosts are spirits that communicate from within the same room as their mediums rather than transmitting messages from some other afterlife location. How can ghosts be here on earth if a different afterlife exists? Some people believe ghosts take a break from their afterlife to visit earth. Others believe that ghosts are trapped here for a reason, such as the need to communicate an important lesson due to a traumatic death, because they don't know they are dead, or because they have unfinished business here on earth.

If the latter is true, you can see how spirit communication can be very important for ghosts; it brings them resolution to issues which prevent them from moving on to a different afterlife or to reincarnation. This hypothesis is another good reason to encourage spirit communication with your spirit after death. A compassionate spirit communicator can help a spirit clear up any last wishes or misunderstandings. For example, here are some questions you can ask a ghost to try to help them:

- Are you aware that you are dead?

- How did you die? Is there any way I can help resolve any trauma from your death?

- Do you have any unfinished business I can help you complete?

- Are there any messages you would like me to pass to specific living people?

If you have any special concerns or fears about being trapped as a wandering ghost after you die, spirit communication can be a great way to rid yourself of those fears while you are still alive. Simply add one or more of the above questions to your spirit communication worksheet. After your death, your designated medium or whomever else you've chosen to allow to contact you will help your spirit clear up any confusion or unfinished business to release you from any unwanted ties to the earth.

Goddesses, Gods, the Higher Self

I am comforted by a quote from a Wiccan religious poem titled "The Charge of the Goddess" in a segment originally attributed to Aleister Crowley. In it, the Goddess says, "I give unimaginable joys on earth; certainty, not faith, while in life, upon death; peace unutterable, rest, ecstasy." To me, this poetry confirms my beliefs that spirit communication is a gift from the divine that gives us certainty of life after death. My God, after all, is the lord of death and resurrection, and he brings comfort and consolation at death. Spirit communication also serves the dead, allowing them to share their peace and ecstasy with the living.

My Gods also help me understand why death exists. In one religious story, my Goddess asks my God why he causes all the things that she loves to die. In response, he tells her that sometimes age and fate are beyond his power, but he offers his strength and peace to the dead as they rest and prepare for reincarnation. Other faith traditions have a more permanent afterlife that serves as the goal for all who die.

For many, the idea of an afterlife is inextricably bound to the idea of a source of higher power. What does this have to do with spirit communication? Well, for some there is no spirit communication without a god or gods as intermediaries or a source of power. That is why it may be important to honor deities (your own or those of the deceased) during spirit communication. You don't have to believe in God to communicate with spirits, but some acknowledgement of a source of power greater than your own may be useful. Think of it like a driver's license. You don't physically *need* a license to drive a car, but it is probably a good idea. You can conceptualize deity as the best expression of yourself or your higher self if external deities don't feel right to you.

Cultures in Which the Dead Begin to Achieve Powerful Status

Let me tell you the story of a person named Lisa. Lisa felt like she was the world's worst goddess worshipper. She always wanted to connect with the divine feminine, but simply could not. She already had a strong relationship with God as a masculine deity through her Christian upbringing. Whenever she tried to imagine a goddess in her life, it seemed fake. Like she was just dressing up God as a woman. To make things more difficult, Lisa was a woman of color, so it seemed like she was forced to choose between paintings and statues of pregnant white goddesses or goddesses from foreign cultures with which she could feel a connection.

It wasn't until she gave birth to her first child that she really felt a connection with the idea of the divine feminine, and then something else happened: Her mother died. Lisa had always been close with her mom, and was devastated that she died before her grandchild could even meet and remember her. Something positive did come out of the process for Lisa, however. Now she had the perfect imagery for a Mother Goddess that made sense.

Instead of hanging a painting on her altar, Lisa propped up a photo of her mom in which she was smiling and laughing. The more Lisa thought about it, the more she realized that her mother had divine qualities of nurturing, love, beauty, kindness, honor, and power. Through her mother, Lisa had been close to the idea of a goddess all along. After the death of her mother, Lisa had no problem praying to the great Mother Goddess, because now that divine woman had a face and a name that were familiar.

Some spirits appear for more than one person, and I mean for this book to be an instruction manual for how to make your spirit appear for more than one person. When your spirit starts branching out and making relationships with complete strangers, you might cease to be simply the spirit of yourself and begin to become the spirit of *something*. You might do well to decide what sorts of people, concepts, and causes you would prefer to represent throughout your spirit existence.

For example, I once worked as a counselor for a residential facility that had a ghost. I normally worked at another location, but I went to the haunted facility for a day to attend a training session. As soon as I arrived, I heard stories about the ghost from some of the residents and even saw him myself. When I told one of the regular staff about my sighting and the rumors, she was almost defensive in response. "Yes, I've seen him," she said. "What of it?" When I remarked that I thought the spirit presence was fun and amazing, she relaxed and told me stories about how he would make pots and pans clatter to the floor in the kitchen just to be a prankster during her night shifts.

After my training, I returned to my regular facility to work and told one of the residents there the story of my sighting. "Oh yeah," he remarked casually, "That's Jim." He had recognized my description of the ghost that was known company-wide as a trickster.

I've already told some stories about how my father's spirit has appeared for his daughter and for his wife during times of stress and worry to comfort and defend us. But he also appeared for my friend, who never considered herself a spirit communicator and who had no special ties to my father. She felt his spirit as a protective force. Even some of my covenmates, friends, and spiritual peers, having never met my father, met and successfully described his spirit's appearance and personality when we celebrated the dead on Samhain. Imagine what would happen if more people collected stories of his spirit appearing as a shielding father figure. These are the sorts of stories that cause spirits to become legends and legends to become myths. This is the sort of afterlife to which I aspire.

What if you could be elevated in status after your death, revered by many? It is not megalomania to believe that such a promotion in your posthumous job description is possible. In fact, ancestors becoming greater through spirit communication happens in many cultures. If you build spirit communication into your wishes after death, you can achieve this incredible way to bless your family line and humanity as a whole for generations to come.

Saints—There is a long process for determining sainthood in the Catholic faith that involves confirmation of miracles. Miracles are exactly the sort of magic or blessings that you will outline in chapter 4 for wishes after your death. For example, if you already agree that you want to aid your family by bestowing healing as a spirit, theoretically those healings could be considered miracles by some. Saints have achieved their saintly status by having those miracles verified by the Catholic church.

Orisha—In Yoruba cultures, there is only one God, but there are many entities that rise almost to the level of deities called Orisha. Orisha may have once been living, but now each represent much more than any human could represent. They have become symbolic archetypes of the personality traits that have been ascribed to them. The Orisha are often called upon to help out living people because they are more relatable and accessible than the omnipotence and transcendence of God.

Lwa—For Vodou practitioners, the Lwa (sometimes called Loa) are a bit of a combination between Catholic saints and West African Orisha, created as a result of slavery in the Americas. When people die, they might start out as one of the Ghede. The Ghede spirits are fun-loving but profane spirits, who are known more for their perverse jokes than they are for individual personalities. After all, the dead don't have to worry about propriety anymore. Over time, spirits may attain the status of Lwa, representing a much more recognizable personality and power just like an Orisha.

This sort of elevated status in other cultures is not farfetched in our own. Many interactions with spirits take on a sort of blessing component, so that other people might travel great distances even to interact with the spirit of a place that can provide healing or abundant wealth or, in the case of my future spirit existence, tell fortunes. When I was a child, there was a spirit who was thought to live in the forest near my home that could bless relationships and give them the potential to last longer.

Teenagers in the neighborhood would take their boyfriends or girlfriends out to that wooded place to ask the spirit to bless their relationships with loyalty and longevity. A sighting of the spirit was thought to be a sign that their prayers would be answered. If instead there was nothing but the ominous sounds of the forest, the relationship was doomed to failure. The spirit was nothing more than the supposed ghost of a local housewife, but she had been elevated to a high status among the teens, who referred to her only by the title of "Love Ghost." She was spoken about with reverence.

How Can You be Sure? Developing Strong Faith

When I act in my role as a hospital chaplain, I admire those who go to their deaths with faith and anticipation. One woman with a brain tumor prayed up until her dying day. She was smiling, blissful, and at peace. She told her family she would watch over them in spirit and promised to always protect her grandchildren. When one niece was crying at her bedside, she told the girl that she would watch over her wedding in spirit. When she lapsed into a coma, that same peaceful smile was on her lips. She had asked for spiritual music to be played as her life-support systems were removed, so I did so. Her family members said that they could see her spirit leave her body, and they spoke quietly afterwards about how happy they were that she was free from the confines of a feeble and pain-ridden body.

You too can develop a faith so strong that death might be a more peaceful process for you and your family. The first step is to make spirit communication a regular part of your life and to share it with your family members. Not only will you be preparing for your spirit's existence after death, but you will also be gaining faith through your own experience. It is one thing to read stories about spirits on a page, but quite another to see and hear spirits with your own eyes and ears. Seeing is believing, and you can share the beliefs that have endured across time and immeasurable distance in this world.

Spirit communication is a great commitment of time and bravery if you are new to it. You'll have to try very hard, and you might have some sessions that are more successful than others. Devote yourself to the task in the same way you might dedicate yourself to any other serious spiritual, mental, or physical discipline.

The final step to developing a strong faith is learning how to articulate it, if only to yourself. Being able to construct a coherent belief system in your mind is easier said than done, however. It is challenging to think about these deep and complex topics. In the next section, I'll instruct you on how to write your own statement of faith. If you find it difficult, it can be helpful to review the written spirit messages you have received. Some important points may be reiterated over and over again. An extremely common example is the topic of love. Many spirits focus on transmitting messages of love, so their mediums over time may follow a faith where love is a central precept. You may find other recurring themes in your spirit messages. Your statement of faith doesn't have to be the product of a movement that informs millions. It can be simply a solid expression of your own inner wisdom. You can pull out relevant portions of your statement of faith to add to the brief statement of faith in chapter 4.

A Long-form Statement of Faith

A good place to start is with your religious history. Not only is your past an important part of your story, but this can help clear up some misconceptions, especially if you or your family members are operating under the assumption that you are still practicing the religion of your childhood. In reality things may have changed. Start with a chronological timeline of your religious identification or culture of origin. If you have made a transition to a new faith (or out of an old one), note that clearly in your story.

Next might be the hard part. Solidify what you believe in right at this moment. To brainstorm this part of your long-form statement of faith, turn to your notes or journal from your spirit communication experiences. If your journal isn't handy or if it is incomplete, you can start by jotting down some specific memories of spirit communication experiences on a separate sheet of paper. Returning to your statement of faith, start writing down only the things about which you are certain. For example, you might start by saying, "I believe that my existence continues after death." Or you might state "I believe in spirit communication after death." If you have strong beliefs about deity, reincarnation, heaven, or any other religious ideas, you can include those as simple statements as well. What do you suppose will happen to you immediately after you die? Who will you meet? What challenges or joys will happen to you?

Next, think about how you feel when somebody else dies. What beliefs would help you to process the event? When you die, what words of comfort would you want to offer your loved ones? This section of your statement of faith should be written while keeping in mind which of your beliefs might be nourishing for other people. Some examples might include a belief that the afterlife is without suffering or that you believe that you will meet your loved ones again after reincarnation. And of course, you can include a reminder that they can contact you through spirit communication, especially if you want to offer advice or help as a spirit.

Finally, make sure you include some practical notes about how your beliefs affect your final arrangements. In my example, I said that I wanted to be cremated after death to symbolically speed transformation from the physical world into the spiritual. Another example would be to write that organ donation would be a spiritual expression of the continuation of life after death. If you have specific burial or funerary traditions from your religion, you can add those here. These concrete steps will give people some easy ways to honor your faith.

When you have finished your statement of faith, make sure you review it at regular points in your life. You might want to put it in a scrapbook or journal that is likely to be flipped through during holidays or at your birthday. Make sure to look to your statement of faith after major life events like marriage or having a child. These events might affect (and add to) the complexity of how you understand your faith. You don't have to include your long-form statement of faith in your last wishes if you want to keep most of it private, but you should draw from the practical portions to leave specific instructions behind. Your statement of faith as a whole can be left as a special legacy so that people can understand the deepest parts of your heart after you are gone. This understanding can also facilitate communication with your spirit.

Things to Consider

1. Have a partner read over your statement of faith (or you can read it yourself) trying to feel the perspective of another person. What feelings are evoked by your statement of faith? What did you write that is comforting? What did you write that seemed confusing or vague?

2. Come up with a prayer, mantra, or daily affirmation you can say that aligns with your beliefs regarding life after death and spirit communication.

3. Did a particular experience in your life cause you to believe what you do now? Retell one important life experience, and think about how it has influenced you.

4. What is one thing you are certain about spiritually? Write it down or create a piece of art to remind yourself of it and place it somewhere in your home.

5. Think of or find somebody who has beliefs that are different than yours. Together, try to find some similarities in your belief systems.

CHAPTER FOUR

Your Wishes for Communicating After Death: A Workbook

This chapter is the most important part of this book, because it will help you think through and create your own wishes for after you are gone. I will give extensive instructions for each of the sections of the workbook first, with examples, so that you know exactly what you need to do. Use a blank sheet of paper, create a document on your computer, or go to my website and download a blank worksheet at www.earthshod.com/worksheet. This section will be followed by a completed example form so that you will see how it should look.

When to Make Plans

I strongly feel that you should do this now, and tell people about it! It is never too early to complete your plans for how people can talk to you after you're gone. It is also a very good idea to communicate the mundane details of end-of-life matters. Most people don't take the simple steps that can prevent needless confusion and additional suffering while also grieving. So do this right now without any more excuses. Grab a chair and start typing. You can also make a photocopy of the form near the end of this chapter and continue your answers on scrap paper, or if you think you have enough room, simply pencil in your answers as you go, straight onto the page. It is okay to pause in the middle and come back if you are interrupted.

It is also important to tell people about your plans, in person, in words. When you die, your loved ones are going to be scrambling like crazy. Even if you leave everything spelled out in various forms, they will remember your kind voice imparting important information with more conviction than they will trust any document. I plan to leave each of my own children a well-worn copy of this book, tied in a red ribbon with many notes written in the margins. However, my death day will certainly not be the first time that they lay eyes on this book.

If you have trouble thinking of ways to discuss this sort of thing with younger children and family members, return to the first chapter of this book to begin transforming death into a more positive part of the magic of life in your family. To reduce awkwardness with other adults, more help with how to talk with you after you are gone is included in chapter 5. For now, just focus on pushing aside any emotional avoidance that would prevent you from starting on this workbook right this minute.

Your Information

Start out by listing some basic information about you that might be used to spiritually address you. Your heirs might want to do genealogy research and that can be difficult if they don't have basic information about you, such as your birth name, any name changes, your date of marriage, and the names of significant relatives such as your parents and children. Include not only your birth date, but your place of birth and your time of birth, if known. That way, astrological charts can be done to analyze your personality even after death. Make sure to list any significant nicknames or spiritual names you have, in case those names come up when people contact you.

For example, my full legal name is Alexandra Nicole Chauran, but during my life I have been called anything from "Nikki" to "Alex" to "Doc." If somebody was trying to talk to me as a spirit and received the name "Doc," the person may have no idea that the spirit is me unless I told them about that name. Through some methods of spirit communication, short words like nicknames may be far more easily transmitted by spirits than long legal names that are difficult to spell.

Your Beliefs Background:
A Statement of Faith

You don't have to adhere to one particular faith or label your faith as a denomination to write a statement of faith. The whole point of writing a statement is that you are stating your personal beliefs and attitudes about spirit communication. It may be your own unique religion that uses a bunch of different existing religions as a basis. Your faith may be completely individual, and that's just fine.

Your loved ones will want to respect your beliefs. To do that, they'll have to know a little bit more about what you believe. Beliefs surrounding death are extremely varied. For example, a Catholic person might be horrified if they were cremated instead of buried. Another problem can arise when rituals are performed without permission. Within the Church of Jesus Christ of Latter Day Saints, members' ancestors can be converted post-mortem. That is, they are offered the chance to choose the Mormon religion after death. Some people might feel very insulted by that possibility, so if you have Mormon relatives, you might want to include a statement declining post-mortem conversion in your statement of faith. Both Catholics and Mormons would be offended by Satanist (Church of Satan) prayers.

As an example, I'll state my beliefs; they are unusual and people might make assumptions about them. I am a Wiccan. As such, I would not be offended by cremation as some faith traditions might, and in fact, I would prefer cremation due to my belief in the magically transformational properties of the element of fire. As a witch, I would not be annoyed at the thought of somebody dancing naked on my grave, but I would want to be addressed respectfully even after I am gone. Unlike members of other faith traditions, I might enjoy the trappings of ritual as a spirit, so offerings such as incense might be appropriate. More specifics about those appear later in this chapter, under "Offerings."

If you are still not sure about what you believe, don't feel daunted. Write down only what you know right now. In chapter 5, we'll explore your beliefs in more depth. At that time, you may find yourself adding to what you have here already. Think of this as a working document in progress that might need further review as you grow and develop as a human being. Start by naming your denomination, if any, and any deities you may believe in. If there are specific practices antithetical to your beliefs, you can name them as well and ask that they not be included in your spirit communications sessions.

Proving You're *You*

Houdini left a secret message to his wife to ensure that she would not be fooled after his death by untrustworthy mediums. The code was supposedly a ten-word cryptogram beginning with the name of a song his wife sang in her vaudeville act. The secret code went: "Rosabelle. Answer, tell, pray, answer, look, tell, answer, answer, tell." Supposedly, the code corresponded to letters of the alphabet and spelled out the word "BELIEVE." Houdini's wife simply knew that there would be a ten-word code, and that it would mean "Rosabelle, believe." You don't have to do anything as complex, but you certainly have the option to make the same plans for your own family. If you don't let sneaky tricksters look over your shoulder while you fill out your worksheet, you can leave your own answer in code, or as a story or fact that only you and a loved one would know.

Who Can Contact You?

I don't force any spirits to talk to me. The only spirits who want to communicate with me are those who have chosen to do so. That said, I have had some spirits who have declined to talk with me when I call them, either by responding with silence or responding with a vehement "no."

When I talk to somebody who is dead I am often talking to a loved one; however, the vast majority of the spirits I have contacted up to now have been strangers. This is merely because I am a professional fortune teller, and my work as a medium has afforded me the opportunity to be invited to contact many people who I never knew when they were living. Through the course of connecting with those spirits, I have learned more about who they were in life and what sort of experience they are having after death. In some cases, I feel that I have even been able to help them by connecting them with their living relatives or otherwise being the hands and feet in the world that they no longer have.

Would you want anybody off the street to be able to invoke your ghost from beyond the grave, or do you want it to be a special and intimate experience for loved ones only? Specify clearly who you want to be able to contact you. You can name specific people, such as your best friend or spouse, or you can decide on a genetic line, such as your children and all their future progeny.

As for myself, I'll be glad to make my spirit available to anyone after death. Not only will it help my memory live on, letting more people get to know who I was during this life, but it may give me more opportunities to help others than I was given during life. Choose carefully whether you'd like to invite just anyone to talk with you after death. As a spirit, you'll certainly have a choice whether to respond when somebody requests your presence, but it will greatly enhance your chances of being called up after death if you ask specific people to do so.

Intensity and Purpose for After-death Interactions

When my best friend was house-sitting for me after my dad's death, she suddenly got a very creepy feeling that somebody was watching her. A very logical and agnostic person, she wasn't usually given to superstitions or spiritual wonderings, so she tried to calm herself down with the assumption that it was just anxiety. Lying down on the couch to relax, she glanced upward into a shiny lampshade and saw the reflection of a man standing in the hallway that she recognized to be the ghost of my deceased father. "It's just me, house-sitting," she said. "Don't hurt me, Mr. Pawlucki!" The ghost reflection disappeared, but she could still sense his presence. Now that's one intense interaction with a ghost! My father presented as a protective spirit that materialized right in front of a person who didn't even call for him. That might not be the sort of thing that you envision for yourself. As a spirit, you might like to talk to people without intimidating them, appearing out of the blue as a specter. Just what sort of intensity, purpose, or type of interactions do you want after death?

These follow-up questions depend greatly on your own belief system after death and your own cultural ideas about what role death should play in the thoughts and lives of your descendants. Think carefully about what you believe. Do you believe there will be a paradise after death? Will there be a queue waiting for reincarnation? Do you believe that your sole purpose in the afterlife will be to wait on a cloud watching over and helping out with your loved ones' earthly woes?

It is also important to consult your belief systems with regard to magic. Magic is the art of changing the universe to match what somebody wills it to be. The living can ask for the aid of spirits to carry out their magical will. Some belief systems strictly prohibit the use of magic. If you feel it would be wrong for you to help your loved ones perform magic, you should specify that you just want to chat with your loved ones after your death or go so far as to offer advice on life.

If, however, you believe in magic and support its use, you can specify how you might want to offer magical help as a spirit. For example, you can offer spiritual protection to your loved ones or aid in earthly troubles such as looking for job opportunities or an appropriate lover. Do you want to be contacted for advice when people make major decisions in life? Would you mind if somebody summoned your spirit when feeling bored or lonely?

Obviously, there are plenty of values to consider here. Decide first whether you believe spirits have better things to do than to satisfy the boredom and curiosity of anyone who contacts them. Personally, I look forward to being at the beck and call of such people after death, but others might find the idea undignified or even profane.

Think carefully, too, about how your loved ones are likely to react after your death. Is your child, spouse, or mom an independent person who will be sad for a while but able to function after you die? If so, you needn't worry about him or her postponing decisions until checking in with your spirit after your death. These days I am lucky enough to have people in my life who would only use spirit communication appropriately, and are not likely to use it as a crutch to avoid the grieving process. However, if one of your loved ones tends to be clingy, you might want to set some boundaries and say that you're only there after death to chat, not to micro-manage their affairs.

Prevent Spiritual Negative Use

Most people try to contact spirits for positive purposes; as confirmation that there is life after death, reconnection with someone they dearly miss, or curiosity. However, there are magical practitioners who try to use spirits for negative purposes. As a professional fortune teller, I've come across many clients who believe that spirits have been used against them. One client believed that an ex-girlfriend was a witch who was sending the spirits of dead people to spy on him and see whether he had a new love. Another client believed that the spirit of the mother of an ex-boyfriend was sent by him to prevent her from finding true love by scaring off new boyfriends, and possibly even trying to harm her by sabotaging her car and causing mechanical difficulties.

It is important to note that these cases are incredibly rare, and the reason is twofold. Firstly, it is highly unlikely that the average person who wants to commit harmful acts would have the basic spirit communication skills necessary to do so, such as those outlined in chapter 2. Secondly, most spirits simply wouldn't be on board with the idea of spending their eternity making some stranger's life miserable. Those who actually command spirits are few and far between, so, as a spirit, if somebody did ask something of you, you could easily decline.

The best way to prevent people from even asking questions you don't want to deal with is to outline what you find morally reprehensible or ethically grey. For instance, I would make sure that my loved ones knew I wouldn't want to be used in magic that would harm anyone unless it were in defense of immediate harm. I also personally wouldn't want to be called on in love spells that force one person to love another. The latter smacks of interference with free will, which feels wrong.

Leaving behind an "or else" clause

Luckily, you can also work to prevent the extremely unusual case in which an experienced magical practitioner who can actually command spirits gets a hold of your spirit for nefarious purposes. You can simply address him or her with an "or else" clause that supplies the consequences you feel come from sending such negative energies into the universe. It is sometimes thought that these "or else" clauses are curses, and they certainly do qualify, in a roundabout way.

For one thing, you won't be the one cursing. It was thought that King Tut's tomb was cursed by his spirit, because of the horrible things that happened to the people who disturbed his final resting place; he didn't even leave a written curse. The discoverers of the tomb reportedly felt very strongly that their presence was unwelcomed, and their full knowledge of that fact allowed the spiritual consequences of such an act to more smoothly and quickly bring about the natural results from the universe.

Think of the "or else" clause as a warning that will make a potential perpetrator fully aware and informed about the swift consequences that will follow any actions. Of course, the nature of those consequences will be dependent upon one's own personal beliefs. One person might believe that such evil acts would result in a trip to hell, while another person who doesn't believe in hell might think that the negativity would simply be revisited upon the person who committed the crime. Here are some examples of "or else" clauses that might be left by different people.

- "My spirit shall not be used for any magic spells, or else the magical practitioner will suffer the consequences of hell for going against the will of God."

- "My spirit will not be used to control somebody else's will, or else the controller will find himself or herself stuck in the cycle of death and rebirth eternally for not learning this important lesson."

- "My spirit will not be used to harm others, or else such harm will return to the culprit three times."

Such a clause may seem cruel or scary, but it is actually a warning that you should leave for anybody you care about. Chances are that any sort of negativity that a person does will harm them in some way or another. So if you can warn about what might happen and hopefully prevent such action from being taken, you will be doing people a favor. Take care to deliver the message seriously and clearly, rather than candy-coating it.

Methods of Interaction

There are many methods that one can use for spirit communication. Several such techniques are shared in chapter 2. For now, I will break the methods down into several categories so you can start to get a feel for how you might want your relationship with your loved ones to proceed after you are done.

There are a few things to consider as you go over this list. First, think about whether any of your beliefs will limit the use of some techniques. For example, some religious texts specifically forbid divination, which is one method of spirit communication. Think about what will be most convenient, simple, or fulfilling for the people who will be talking to you. A very spiritual younger sister might be delighted and inspired to learn a complex divination technique that could be too complex or confusing for an elderly spouse. Your average everyday person might appreciate an extremely simple technique, while a child of yours might feel limited by the more simple method's limited information. Think about your audience as you survey the following basics, and remember that you can choose more than one.

Direct Communication

The first category of communication is called direct because it does not require any tools, and you might even get literal messages given directly to you. The limitations of these methods is that they require a good deal of concentration and effort, and some people may find it hard to receive any detailed message at all. However, they don't require you to prepare any supplies and the messages may feel less complex or confusing for some people.

Dreams—After you die, your loved ones can ask
   for you to appear to them in their dreams. The
   benefits of dreaming for spirit communication
   are manifold. After all, everybody already sleeps
   and dreams, so this method can feel the most
   comfortable to people who are leery of spirit
   communication. There is a firm boundary between
   sleep and wakefulness, so you won't have to worry
   about taking up too much of your loved one's time
   or interfering with the grieving process by causing
   an obsession. In a dream, a spirit can appear and
   speak or interact just as they did in life.

Omens—Omens are real things that you see, hear, or
   experience that have meaning ascribed to them. For
   your purposes, you can tell your loved ones to watch
   for specific omens. Typically, traditional omens
   might include the bark of a dog, the chirping of a
   specific species of bird, or the sounds of frogs or
   crickets. You could pick even more rare events such
   as double rainbows or formations of clouds or birds.

Clairsentience—You know that feeling when deep inside
   your mind and soul you simply know something

is true? That feeling of certainty, when it is spot on, is called clairsentience, and it can be applied to knowing what a deceased loved one has to say or think about you. You can invoke clairsentience through trance meditation. Sometimes, mental pictures of a deceased loved one may appear—this is called clairvoyance. Sometimes, you might mentally hear the voice of a loved one, and that is called clairaudience. Note that you might not literally hear the person's voice but instead "hear" it the same way that you hear a song stuck in your head.

Channeling and Possession—This is the most advanced of the direct methods of spirit communication. In channeling or possession, the spirit enters the body of the living person and speaks or performs actions directly through his or her body. "Channeling" is the word used to describe the process when the purpose is passing along a message through speaking or writing. Possession implies a more complete takeover of the body's faculties so that the spirit can experience life again. The term for retaining complete awareness when a spirit gives messages through your voice is "overshadowing." Channeling and possession often require two living people to get the message across from the spirit; one person should channel the message and the other listen and record it, since the possessed person may not have enough awareness or presence of mind to remember the message.

Adding Simple Tools

Adding some simple tools to the mix can help make the message more clear without making things too complicated for the loved one trying to talk with the spirit. Before we get into some more complex methods of divination that can render a rich and clear message with a little bit of skill development, I'd like to go over a few more simple tools. Anyone can obtain them and use them easily.

Automatic Writing—Necessitating only a pen and paper, automatic writing is an extension of channeling. When automatic writing, a spirit controls a living person's hand such that the message from the spirit is transmitted directly to the paper. The benefit of automatic writing is that it reduces the necessary number of participants for channeling to one. Automatic writing can be challenging, because some people will need to be in a trance state, which can take some time and skill or natural talent.

Yes/No Stones—Find a flat stone and paint "yes" on one side and "no" on the other. Simple, binary answers can be found by placing the stone inside a bag, and fishing it out of the bag without looking. This method requires no trance state or skills, and the stone can be easily fashioned with ordinary supplies and any flat rock. Of course, the binary answers are the limitations of this method. More is given about the "yes/no" stone in the crash course instruction chapter on spirit communication.

Spirit Board—A Spirit Board (usually called a Ouija
　　Board) is a cardboard game board on which all of the
　　letters of the alphabet appear along with the numbers
　　0–9 and the answers "yes," "no," and "goodbye." It
　　comes with a planchette, which is a small plastic lens
　　that can be moved across the board by hand to spell
　　out messages from the spirit, in a similar channeling
　　method to automatic writing. You can purchase your
　　own spirit board, or you can make one using a piece
　　of paper, pen, and an overturned glass. More about
　　using a spirit board is included in chapter 3.

Divination

Divination is a way to communicate with spirits through
tools that have a generally agreed-upon function and set of
meanings. In fact, the simple tools above could be considered a basic form of divination. There are countless forms
of divination enjoyed across many cultures. I will list a few
common favorites below that might strike your fancy.

Tarot—The tarot is a deck of seventy-eight cards, each
　　of which has a particular meaning. When laid out
　　in order, the tarot cards tell a classic story of the
　　archetypical hero's journey, the adventure of the
　　human condition. When randomly laid out in
　　configurations called spreads, the cards can tell the
　　story of the message of a spirit. The benefit of tarot
　　cards is that the meanings have been fully studied
　　and explored, so you can often be more certain of

what is said. The limitation of tarot cards is that they won't be able to give meanings not found in the cards, for example they cannot spell a name.

This is not to say that tarot cards cannot be used for spirit communication. In fact, tarot cards were used during one of my first spirit communication attempts for somebody outside of my circle of friends and family. I was a young college student, reading tarot cards at a campus fundraiser for my Pagan student group. I was proud to be a founder of the first Pagan student group at the University of Washington and giddy with the idea of accepting money for such a service for the first time, overjoyed to receive such gratitude from my new "clients" and even a few generous tips. A mother and her college-aged daughter approached my table. The daughter was in tears. The mother explained that the love of her life and the father of her beautiful daughter had just died, and that her daughter had been watching my table for some time, hoping to get a reading on him but too nervous to approach. Aside from nodding, the younger woman said nothing, but her eyes were full of emotion.

I was nervous about accepting such a responsibility, especially since reading for strangers was so new to me. I tried to talk her out of it, saying that I didn't want to affect her grief process and that this was too public a venue for such a private and intimate matter. As the more experienced and cautious person I am today, I probably wouldn't have chanced the reading at all, but in that moment when I looked into my peer's eyes and saw the mixture of hurt and hope, I was powerless to resist.

I laid out the cards and began reading the meanings, and the mother and daughter pair broke out in happy sobs. Not only did my interpretation make sense to them, but the deck that I was using had a court card called "Princess," her father's pet name for her, and all four of the Princess cards came out at once right away. To those hopeful ears, they were his voice calling out, "Princess, princess, princess, princess…" Maybe tarot cards aren't always the most clear with their spirit communications, but that pair of women had been guided to tarot cards that day because they held the message they needed to hear.

Casting bones, sticks, or stones—The practice of casting lots is found in nearly every culture. Objects are put into a bag and then scattered randomly on the ground and interpreted where they lie. Sometimes markings are added: to stones to make them runes, to sticks to make them ogham. When read in conjunction with the way they lie, markings can enrich the meaning of the message, but they aren't necessary.

Every year at Samhain, I like to cast the bones to get a general message from spirits. At one point before I had children, I cast the bones to ask my ancestors their opinion about me procreating, since I was nervous about becoming a mother. A fistful of old dried bones I had collected outdoors through the years fell amazingly into a series of perfect plus-signs, as if they were my own ancient pregnancy test. I took it as a positive sign, encouraging me that my ancestors were enthusiastic about my new venture into parenting.

Scrying—Scrying is a type of divination that involves gazing into a tool until pictures form either in the mind's eye or are identified in the tool. If you have ever been able to see shapes in the clouds in the sky, you can perform scrying. Scrying can be done in a crystal ball, a bowl of water or milk, a tea cup, hot coals, or a candle's flame. Scrying can be the most challenging method of divination, because some people have difficulty seeing identifiable shapes in the tool and then assigning meaning. However, scrying is also the most powerful form of divination, in my opinion, because the messages that can come through are limitless. In a scrying tool, you might even get to see the face of a beloved loved one who has passed on.

When I have performed scrying readings for others, I am surprised by how often I can describe a person that I see and have the description match a deceased loved one that my client is hoping to contact. On one occasion, a client talked me into doing a reading on a deceased grandfather, explaining that it had been a long time since his death and that she wouldn't be traumatized if he appeared in the crystal ball. When he did, his description for her matched perfectly, but that wasn't all. I was also able to describe a cabin in the woods that I saw, along with his old car, which were all memories from the childhood she spent with him. She burst into tears of joy, and for a moment I thought that I really was causing her a lot of grief. She was excited and even a little bit spooked about how well the reading gave her confirmation of her grandfather's presence.

Now that you've seen a few examples of divination, I'll help you through my thought process when I decided how I would like people to talk to me after I am gone. Since I know I'd want anybody off the street to be able to talk to me, I won't be specifically mentioning something that requires concentration or training like the tarot or a scrying method, even though I would certainly allow it. After all, my children and grandchildren will probably be interested in divination because of my work life. But when choosing a tool to request, I would need one that could interest both beginners and advanced spirit communicators alike. Therefore, I have chosen the spirit board as my preferred divination tool, although I will gladly allow others if the person contacting my spirit has a preference.

How Often?

Think about how often you would like to be contacted, considering both whether you believe that spirits have better things to do as well as the effect on the lives of those contacting you. You already have begun thinking about how talking to your spirit will fit into the lives of your loved ones when you decided whether you wanted to just chat or offer advice and aid. Now, combine that picture with your preferred divination method and your belief system to find out what you find reasonable for frequency of communication.

For example, if you believe in a heavenly afterlife and have selected a complex method of divination such as trance scrying, it would probably not be very reasonable to ask to be contacted every day. Imagine being pulled away from a heavenly paradise for a perfunctory communication session. And imagine your child or grandchild pulling away from a family or job because he or she feels obligated to honor you for hours each day. Obviously, balance must be struck between never talking and allowing spirit communication to become rote.

If you want to be contacted only once a year to make it special, think about what would be your special day. If you have chosen only one person to contact you, is there any date that has meaning for you? For a spouse, it could be the month and day of your first date. For a group of relatives, you might suggest your death date, as that would be common knowledge among them, but would discourage just anyone who stumbled across your final wishes. They would be forced to search through records before they could disturb your rest.

If you want just anyone to contact you, your birth date would be a good time. Or, you could select specific holidays, such as the days mentioned earlier in the first chapter on honoring ancestors. I always feel a special connection with the spirit of my Uncle Ron near the winter holidays because he would always come and stay at our home, and it feels like his spirit has continued that tradition. The day that is always special for my father and me is New Year's Eve. When my dad was a young man, his dad always called him on New Year's Eve no matter what the life circumstances. When I grew up, my dad carried on that tradition with me. Even after he was diagnosed with cancer and knew he would die, he promised me that he would always call on New Year's Eve no matter where my life took me. Sure enough, the first New Year's Eve after his death, his spirit "called" me, and we talked. I still remember him every year on New Year's Eve, and I know he calls me to speak to me at that time even more so than on his birth or death date.

Since I am hoping to let everyone contact me, I would choose my birthday as a special day to contact me. However, I don't mind the idea of being contacted frequently after death through simple tools like the spirit board, so I would also encourage the Beltane and Samhain holidays, as well as any full moon for contact. Full moons often aid spirit communication and divination, so they would be an especially easy time for even beginners to contact myself or any other spirits.

Waiting or Right Away?

After somebody dies, especially if the death is sudden or unexpected, a void fills the heart of loved ones. The very fact that the sun rises on an earth where their beloved no longer lives may feel like an insult. Such people may wish to contact the deceased person right away to share feelings and say goodbye or express any regrets. There may be some spiritual processes that delay contact, however, and might make those first few attempts frustratingly quiet.

The mysterious delay between the moment of death and the ability for a spirit to clearly communicate may be the origin of traditions that span cultures that include days of mourning, long funerary rites, or vigils after the spirit has left the body. If your culture or religious tradition has a waiting period, you should specify it in your wishes so your loved ones won't be frustrated and give up if they attempt to contact you during that time. For some cultures, this mourning period can be up to a year. In my personal experience, three days waiting seems to be ideal for a clear communication session, but you don't have to wait that long if you feel you need to contact sooner.

I remember the day my dad died. I was actually asleep when it happened, and I was having a dream. In my dream, I saw my dad. We were standing together on the runway of an airport. Smiling, he climbed into a small aircraft and waved joyfully from the pilot seat. I could tell that he was excited, brimming with anticipation and a bit of boastful pride at being able to fly. I waved back at him, cheering for him and feeling inspired by his own joy. In front of the plane, I saw a goddess directing him to taxi the airplane forward. She waved two torches to indicate his path of travel, and I realized later that she was Hecate, goddess who lights the way to the underworld. The plane engine revved and the airplane rolled down the runway, gathering speed. I cheered as it took off and then was awakened by the telephone ringing.

In the waking world, I answered the phone. My mother was choking back sobs. She simply said, "he's gone." I spent the rest of the day suffering the shock. The simple event of the sun rising hit me like a slap to the face. How could the world just move along as normal while I was suffering such grief? Luckily, I had a wonderful husband to hold me, and it was a Sunday, so I could spend the day trying to distract myself with relaxation. After a scenic drive, we returned home and my husband asked what he could do to help me for the rest of the evening. I answered, "I think I need to pray alone."

Once I had shut myself into solitude, I went about performing a ritual like the one described in chapter 2. I created a sacred space in which I felt both comforted and powerful through a practice called casting a circle. I felt emotionally overwhelmed, so I spoke aloud in freeform prayer, telling my gods how I felt. All of my mixed feelings poured out; I felt joy that my loved one had experienced such a peaceful death and that I had been able to know him throughout my childhood and young adulthood; anger and despair at his passing and at the fact that I had been so far away from him when it happened.

When I had spoken all the words I had to say, I sat and breathed heavily, allowing my mind to clear so I could meditate. What happened next felt like dreaming even though I was wide awake. Behind my closed eyelids I saw imagery that seemed to have a mind of its own, and I felt like I was in a different place, as if my body was fully involved in the dreaming.

I had been transported to my dad's new home. It was a house I had never seen before, but it clearly was furnished with things he loved. There was a table spread with collectable stamps that he had been poring over, sorting and arranging. The tables were piled high with the sort of books he loved to read. Next to a comfortable looking easy chair was a cup that had previously contained coffee. I glanced around looking for him in the expansive space well lit with windows, and I spotted him through a glass door outside, having a smoke.

I walked outside onto a wooden deck that wrapped around the entire building. Palm trees swayed in the warm breeze and I was suddenly aware on some level that this was like Costa Rica, one of his favorite places to travel. My father turned towards me on the deck and smiled. He looked exactly as he had in his mid-forties, though he had been sixty-two when he died. His hair was still mostly black and when I hugged him, the side of his face felt firm with the youth of those extra decades he had recovered.

It felt good to hug him, and I felt the tears well up. The night before he died I had been in another ritual circle, worshipping with a coven and working magic to help my father's spirit pass. The High Priest of that event had hugged me after the ritual and confided that he had lost his own mother earlier that week. He promised me that I would see my dad again as a spirit and that it would be exactly the same as when he was alive except the hugs. But in that moment, even the hugs were the same, and I was awash with relief and validation in my beliefs.

My dad and I sat in deck chairs and watched the palm trees. His home had a lovely view of a beach, and the ocean churned and roared to meet the overcast sky. I felt obligated to catch my dad up on the things happening in the living world, even though part of me assumed he could see everything. I told him that my mom was all right, and that his friends had arrived in time to take care of her after his death so that she would be cared for, urged to do things like eat properly and rest. My dad nodded seriously and then caught me up on things. He quickly rattled off a lot of details about his belongings and the nuts and bolts of his passing that he wanted me to relate to my mom. There was information about his collections, what pieces needed to go together to be sold properly, and even mundane information about where paperwork was located and tidbits about banks and whatnot. I felt overwhelmed, wishing that this dream world had a pad of paper and a pen! (This example is a good reason why you should make sure to have your end-of-life plans sorted before you die so that your first spirit communications with your loved ones can be joyous and comforting reunions instead of confusing mundane matters.)

I asked him those classic questions about whether he was happy where he was, even though I felt it was silly since I believe we can keep being challenged after death in a way that isn't always happy; such an afterlife is even better than eternal bliss. He smiled at me with a sense of pride and told me that he was always happy with me and he was keeping busy where he was. I hugged him again and invited him to come and visit me any time in my dreams or waking life. I promised him that I wouldn't be afraid and that it wouldn't make me go crazy. We laughed together, and then I woke up in my sacred space, still seated in meditation.

I rested for a few minutes so I wouldn't be dizzy when I stood up, and then I went through the ritual steps to clean up the sacred space properly and returned to my husband. He asked me if I wanted to go to a restaurant for dinner, obviously still trying to cheer me up. I agreed, figuring that it was a good idea to keep getting out of the house and living life. After we locked up the house and got into the car, I glanced toward the front door of my home and saw my father's spirit as clearly as if he were still alive. He stood on the doorstep, smoking a cigarette, and lifted one arm to salute me as my husband pulled the car out of the driveway. I smiled and saluted back.

Topics of Consultation

This section only applies if you are willing to be asked for advice in a particular area of expertise. You don't have to be a world-renowned authority on a subject for people to want to hear what you have to say. Perhaps you've just made mistakes in life that gave you knowledge about what to warn or encourage. If you are obsessed with a hobby like knitting, you could virtually be a goddess of such weaving and textiles in the afterlife, advising and offering a helping nudge of intuition and luck in the knitter's time of need. If you've had a successful marriage of fifty years or if you've been divorced ten times, the living would want to hear your reflections, regrets, and wisdom about love.

As for me, since I'm a professional fortune teller, I hope to continue my psychic service, reveal the future, and tell fortunes as a spirit guide. Since I am considered an expert in witchcraft in my community, modern witches can contact me when I am a spirit to ask for help or advice on magic and with writing spells. And because I love my family, I would be happy to aid and protect children and marriages from the spirit world. Even my struggles can be an asset once my suffering is over. Since I have suffered from mental illness in this life, perhaps I can offer help as a patron spirit guide for the mentally ill who petition me once I am a spirit.

Consider strongly your strengths and also your struggles in this life. Decide what you value most. If you could volunteer as much as you wanted without having to worry about logistics or money, what causes would earn your attention? As a spirit, you will have all the time in the world at your disposal to pursue your goals to better the world, and you can start now to recruit the hands, feet, eyes, and ears of the living whom you can employ after you are gone.

Offerings

Recalling the first chapter in which bits of the family meal or glasses of water are often offered on altars or shrines to honor ancestors, think ahead to when you will be among those honored. Don't be bashful, but let people know what sort of beautiful honoring gifts can be displayed to please your spirit. Would you like incense burned and flowers in a vase in front of your picture? What is your favorite scent of incense or type of flower? You can even list your favorite food or beverage, if you like.

The more offerings you name that represent who you are in life, the more likely it will be that people will be able to summon the right spirit after your death. The unique requests you make will draw your spirit to the right place and time on earth as you come to see who has collected all the things you like in one spot. Make sure you pick some things that represent the essence of you, not just something that sounds appropriate. List a few potential offerings, so that if one is not available to somebody who wants to talk to you, another can be chosen instead.

For example, I love the scent of frankincense incense; it is also a resin I use for spiritual purposes to cleanse and bless sacred space, so it is meaningful to me. I would love white flowers to be offered to me, since white is a color I wear often in this life, but it doesn't much matter to me what type of flowers are used, as my favorite flowers are childhood favorites like snapdragons, which are only available during the spring. As for food or beverage, I am known among my friends and family for being a connoisseur of bourbon, but if that's unavailable, a cup of black tea will do in a pinch.

My dad was never an incense lover, but he requested a very strange sort of offering. Well, strange in addition to the golden kazoos he requested to have played at his wake. My father was a collector, and when he found out he was not long for this world he suddenly started collecting hell money. Hell money is a packet of colorful phony bank notes that are burned as an offering for the deceased in Chinese tradition. My father amassed quite the collection, including a large hell note in a frame, a cardboard hell credit card, and masses of joss paper bills. After he died, my family burned them all, and we joked that he must be quite wealthy in the afterlife!

Sacred Places

Sacred places have traditionally been a way for humans to be reminded of spirits' presence. However, I'm not saying you should ask your family members to hop a plane to a haunted castle in Europe to get in touch with you. Think smaller. What small moments in life feel sacred because of the location or environment? For example, if you've ever spent quiet moments on a bridge over a river skipping stones, any bridge over any river could be a sacred place to contact you.

Even places inside a home can be meaningful sacred spaces; for example, in front of a hearth with a roaring fire or in the kitchen for those people who enjoy cooking wonderful meals for the family. My own example of a sacred space is any doorway. A doorway is a symbolic liminal or threshold place between two spaces, so it can represent a place between the worlds. Doorways are also a handy place because they are present in every home. In ancient Scottish invocations of deities to see the future, omens were sought when standing braced at the front door looking out at the world.

If the place you would be contacted doesn't seem very important to you, feel free to skip this step. After all, it may directly conflict with some peoples' values, if they hope to be contacted for chatting and advice at any time. Naming a particular space for communication can be limiting if you want your loved ones to be encouraged to chat with you in the car on the way to work, in bed before going to sleep, or any time they miss you. Consider carefully whether naming a sacred space will make spirit communication more special for your spirit or an unnecessary barrier.

Invocation

An invocation is a set of words that can be used to call forth a specific spirit. Think of your invocation as your spiritual phone number that can be dialed to make the right connection. A proper invocation can make up for any of the other things that aren't quite right, like a lack of offerings or the wrong place or timing. Invocations are a way to get the spirit you are calling to sit up and take notice, although the choice to be summoned is still up to the spirit.

For example, we'll take a very simple invocation used in a common childhood game that also makes use of sacred space. The legend of Bloody Mary varies by region, but it is supposedly a ghost who appears in a mirror when her name is repeated. I performed this invocation as a game with my childhood friends. The invocation was very simple. In some cases, one just had to sit in front of a mirror in a dark room, or a room with just one candle lighting it, and repeat the phrase "Bloody Mary" at least three times. In other versions, kids would walk backwards up stairs while chanting the invocation many times and holding a mirror and a candle, incorporating a specific sacred space into the invocation.

The Japanese version of this spooky invocation game is called *hitori kakurenbo,* meaning "one-person hide and seek." In the Japanese game, the spirit is given any name, such as the name of a deceased person. A doll is cut open, emptied of stuffing and filled with a handful of rice and fingernail clippings, then sewn up with red thread. The sacred space is the bathtub, with water drawn. To start the invocation, the person playing the game says, "[My name] is it" three times, runs away, counts to ten, returns and pierces the doll with a sharp object saying "[Spirit's name] is it" three times. The player then hides quietly and listens for words or other impressions from the spirit. When the spirit communication session is ended, the player emerges from hiding and spits a mouthful of sake or salt water at the doll saying "I win" three times.

As you can see, an invocation can be very simple, and made up of as few as two words. It can also be a complex poem with rhyming couplets or a more elaborate exercise. To decide on complexity, think about whether you would like it to be easily remembered, in which case rhyming and brevity are key. If you'd like people to talk to you on only rare occasions, you can make it special with a particularly long and detailed invocation to remind people more about the details of your life. Your invocation can include the list of your expertise or other directives.

When making my invocation, since I want strangers to be able to use it and remember it, I would make it a point to incorporate some things about me such as my name and areas of interest for giving advice. However, I'd also like for it to rhyme and be relatively short so it could be memorized by somebody who might want to consult me on a moment's notice.

Nuts and Bolts

As mentioned earlier, planning the logistics of how your affairs will be dealt with surrounding the end of your life is emotionally unpleasant but necessary. In your documentation of your spiritual wishes, make sure you reference where important papers such as your will and advanced directives might be located. You can also reiterate important things such as your burial or cremation wishes, your hopes for organ donation, and spiritual details of planning a funeral or a wake.

One way to make the process a little less dull and painful is to carefully fold your wishes for spirit communication into the traditional plans. For example, your wake or memorial can include readings of your invocation or your statement of faith. You can include explanations of what you believe when you write about your final wishes. For example, for me cremation is tied directly to my spiritual beliefs because it represents transformation and I believe that it will more quickly free my spirit for communication. I also have strong moral and ethical beliefs surrounding organ donation, so I would include explanations with my decisions. Such explanations will make the process more helpful for you and will also better encourage your loved ones to follow your wishes as they have been given.

Talking to Family
(While Still Alive)

When I first started my internship as a hospital chaplain, there was very little preparation. I started training with a cohort of about a dozen men and women of varied faith traditions, from Franciscan nuns from Vanuatu and a Philippine Catholic priest to a young follower of Gandhi from India. Some already had rigorous training in counseling at seminary school, but others were completely new. After a brief orientation to hospital rules and regulations and how to use the patient record system on the secure computers, we were each given identification cards.

We were told that these identification cards would get us anywhere in the hospitals, even into the most secure and sterile environments, because a chaplain could be needed anywhere at any time. The hospitals we worked in were labyrinths. Almost immediately we were thrown into the task of helping people in violent transitions in their lives, and were doing things like ushering patients and their families newly informed of a terminal illness to an unmarked room designated as the prayer room. I looked at my smiling face on my ID card above the word "Chaplain." On the back of the card was printed the same instructions given to all hospital employees for how to show caring. They included the following bullet point standards of service, paraphrased here:

- Introduce yourself by name, explain your role.
- Offer to help if someone looks lost or confused.
- Assist people to get where they need to go.
- Always ask, "Is there anything else I can do for you?"

Fast forward a couple of weeks later. Nearly half of the people in my clinical pastoral education program had quit. The emotional and spiritual toll exacted by holding the hands of the dying and helping families to walk away from their loved ones for the last time was too much. The spiritual demands required to help staff deal with unexpected paranormal encounters was not the sort of thing they felt ready to handle. I was still there, however, happy with my job and my learning in the program. My remaining colleagues were sharing their disappointment in the level of preparation with our supervisor when I piped up saying that I felt perfectly equipped to help patients and their families. Everyone looked at me as if I'd lost my mind.

I pointed at the back of my name tag. "It's all right here," I said, and recited the bullet points aloud. "Whenever I was paged to see someone, I just followed this handy list like this: Hi, my name is Alex and I'm a chaplain. You look lost and confused. Can I help you? Is there anything else I can do for you?" When the laughter subsided, a vigorous discussion ensued, during which a conclusion was reached that talking about death doesn't require extreme training or preparation, just a willingness to listen and help in whatever manner is needed.

This kind of frank communication is key. Talk about life and death with your family. None of this spirit communication work will be worth anything if you don't discuss it with your loved ones while you are still alive. No matter how much the letter you leave behind tugs at their heartstrings, the fact is that the first few days, weeks, and months after your death will be a whirlwind of confusion and denial for those left behind. Explicit instructions can be ignored or simply missed. A conversation about something you may have wanted many years ago can easily dominate a cold piece of paper in times of emotionally driven decisions.

Make sure your conversations about end-of-life issues are recent and ongoing. That way, old memories of something you may have once said will not override what you truly want. Also, people will more easily match up your documentation of your wishes with memories of your true desires. That means that you're going to have to normalize your concepts of death and spirit communication. For some, that might mean a sort of coming out of the closet, admitting that you believe there is a possibility for your loved ones to talk to you after death.

For me, this process was mostly easy since I have always had alternative spiritual beliefs. However, some dialogues are more challenging than others. I'll go over a few people who will need to be in on your plans, and how you might go about bringing up the topic and keeping it fresh in the minds of everyone who matters.

Spouse

My spouse has always known that I have a spirituality that includes spirit communication. So our talks about what will happen if one or the other of us dies first usually dissolve into jokes about who is going to "haunt" whom. Honestly, though, we trust each other and have standing permission for any sort of magical or spiritual interventions that are well-intentioned in nature.

Hopefully your spouse is already somewhat aware of your spiritual beliefs. If not, you might have a challenging road ahead. If you are in the type of marriage where spiritual beliefs are a "don't ask, don't tell" topic, it is time to break out of that rut. You can start by asking your spouse about his or her own beliefs. It may seem counterintuitive, but the way to start talking with a spouse about these uncomfortable topics is to begin with the hardest but most necessary decisions. Start with any discussions that you need to have about what will happen with your children and belongings if you both should die in the same car accident, for instance. From there, start branching out to explore what differences, if any, the two of you might have in your wishes.

An important topic to bring up is what will happen with remarriage. If your spouse remarries after you die, would you still want to continue a spirit communication relationship, or would you rather that you both move on? Having an ex-wife who is a ghost might interfere with a man's dating prospects, after all, especially if she has a say in things. If, however, the two of you have a quirky relationship or can agree to just be friends after you die, you can come to an agreement. Trust me, a long-distance relationship is especially hard if one of you is dead.

Friends

Friends may be a bit more difficult to talk with about your death if your spouse is your best friend. Why might you want to tell friends about your end-of-life plans? If your entire family were involved in an accident together, you will only have your friends to remember your wishes for you if everyone else is not in a position to articulate your desires. Your friends might also be on a similar wavelength as you, and could be more likely to want to communicate with you immediately after death than a grieving family.

Your friends might not feel ready to discuss their own end-of-life plans, so you might need a different strategy to bring it up. There's no wrong way to stretch and grow your friendship with this special topic, so don't be afraid if you have to bring it up even with an inappropriate joke or two over a couple glasses of wine. However, if you want to be serious about things, you can do so by setting aside time to talk with each of your friends and telling them that you want to share something special about yourself. That sort of mysterious clue will cue your friend that this is not a laughing matter and that you expect to be taken seriously and treated with respect.

When setting up that all-important coffee date with your friend, make sure you've completed the worksheet in this book and perhaps even have a copy of the book for your friend, if he or she is new to the idea of spirit communication. Start by being frank. None of us is going to live this physical life forever, so you've rightfully been thinking about how things are going to be after you are gone. Don't flood your friend with too much information, but have the worksheets and book on hand for curious questions. Even if the person doesn't have anything to say, you can thank your friend for politely bearing with you and offer a copy of your worksheet just for safekeeping. It is good to give out as many copies as you can so that people don't lose track of your spirit communication plans in the flurry of activity surrounding your eventual departure.

If your friend is enthusiastic and intrigued about what you're doing, this is a good time to ask if he or she wants to start learning about spirit communication. The two of you can get together and practice spirit communication, possibly even getting in touch with some mutual friends on the other side. Set up a follow-up date to get together and try out some spirit communication. Your first efforts could take the form of a tame book club or a wild spirit board party.

Invite your friend to help you think of others who would be interested in the topic. If you're hoping that many people will contact you after you're gone, spreading the message is in your best interest. Refer to the "Things to Consider" at the end of each chapter for discussion questions.

Children

Talking about death with children can be tricky. You have the problem of age-appropriate conversations if your kids are very young. The general rule of thumb is to try to explain the concepts of death and spirit communication to children only at the level that they can understand. Allow them to ask questions and answer them as honestly and openly as possible. Since your biological children are always younger and more immature than you, even if they are teens or adults, don't be surprised if your kids aren't yet at your level of embracing spirit communication. Then again, don't be surprised if they are. I once heard my toddler talking animatedly to somebody in her room. When I went to check on her, she had gently taken down a photograph of her deceased Grandpa Roy and was speaking to him. I let her chat a good long while until she was finished. We sat down and talked about Grandpa Roy, said a little prayer, and later read a bedtime story about spirits.

Your first step, if your kids are still living with you, should be to go over the beginning chapter of this book. This can begin to build a healthy attitude towards death and spirit communication in your family. Laying this groundwork will ease the way for difficult conversations and provide opportunities for talking openly about death and what life will be like for your kids after you die. My own children are still babies, but I actually look forward to helping them build a positive and accepting attitude towards death, and I already read to them stories that include spirit communication in a positive way.

If your children are very young, building daily rituals and spaces in which to honor your beloved dead will be important. Avoid brushing off any morbidly curious questions that young children might ask about your death or their deaths. For spirit communication, you can begin praying with your kids if you are comfortable with prayer. Tell your kids that even when you are gone you will still be listening when they talk to you. Help kids start exploring their own beliefs by asking curious questions about what they think happens after somebody dies. If they ask a question you don't know the answer to, admit that you don't know and ask what they think.

If your children are older, they may be exploring their own beliefs about life after death. You'll find it can be more difficult to see eye to eye, especially if you have a rebellious teenager. You won't be able to force your young adult to see your point of view, but you can still share your opinions on the afterlife, and support him or her in reading and learning about what other people believe. Phrase things in terms that describe what you believe rather than those that describe how things are in the world. Presented this way, you can avoid some push back if your teenager doesn't see things the way that you do.

It can be awkward for some kids to talk directly to their parents about difficult matters, even if they are sympathetic to your beliefs. Don't be afraid to enlist the help of your kid's peers or other family members. For example, your kid may not want to summon spirits with his mom, but he might want to have a cool spirit communication party or try having a séance with his wacky aunt. Don't take it personally if your kid doesn't want to involve you right away in his or her explorations of death. It might feel too scary to imagine your death at this stage in his or her level of maturity, so you'll have to be patient and let your child set the pace.

If your child is an adult, be mindful that he or she may still be in the process of building maturity and wisdom. If your adult child is busy with other priorities in life, it can be easy to brush aside your request to talk about deep things like spirit communication. You might have to set up the right time to bring up the topic as an enjoyable way to connect, such as at a Halloween spirit communication family gathering. Try asking your adult child for help with a New Year's resolution to get your life plans together. No matter how much resistance you run into, don't put off the talk too long. Your children will be grateful that you helped them prepare for the changes in life and for a relationship with you beyond death.

Parents

Parents can be a tough group to talk with about death, mostly because parents hope their children will outlive them. However, there may be several reasons why you would want to tell your parents about your plans. If you happen to die suddenly in an accident, your parents might be the ones to act upon many of your wishes, especially if you are not married and don't have adult children. And if you are under eighteen, your parents are legally in charge of making plans for you. You might also simply want to share this special part of your belief system, especially if you hope that they too, will want to communicate after death. We'll go over each of these scenarios in turn.

If your parents are your only next of kin, it is important that you bring up your plans as matter-of-factly as suggested above in the section on telling a spouse. Let your parents know that you've been thinking about the future and you want to hammer out some details. Make a copy of your plans for spirit communication along with the rest of your documents, and be clear about what you want. You can have a copy of this book handy for follow-up questions if they seem curious about your beliefs.

If you've never really been of the same belief system as your parents, or if you feel like you have escaped a repressive belief system that was imposed upon you, these talks will be more difficult. You'll have to reassess why you are having the conversation in the first place. If there are past arguments that need to be rehashed, those conversations may well be reserved for family therapy rather than in the context of talking about your personal plans.

Always be respectful of the beliefs of others, even if you are pretty sure that your parents aren't sincere about their beliefs or if their belief system seems just plain wrong. There is no way that you will be able to force them to believe in spirit communication if it's not their thing. The most heartbreaking situation can develop when you are hoping that they will want to talk to you after they die, and they just refuse. Don't push the issue. Feel free to supply information and share what you believe with them, but be mindful that they can be as set in their ways (if not more so) than you are.

Hopefully all will go well. I know that I am incredibly lucky to have parents who have always supported my exploration of spiritual beliefs. When alive, my atheist father thought that my belief system was, at worst, harmless. My mother, thankfully, is just as sold on the idea of spirit communication as I am. Mom will read this book, of course, so she will learn my point of view in depth and like other parents, misunderstandings and confrontations will be unlikely. We've also had frank discussions about death and lived through the challenge of my father's death together. Consider your own parents' reactions to the death of a loved one when you talk with them.

The Worksheet

Now that we've gone over all the things you should be thinking about as you plan, it is time for you to complete the worksheet. Grab a pencil and paper and get started! Fill it in without worrying about whether you're writing your final answers or whether you'll have time to complete the whole thing. This is a rough draft because there is no such thing as a final draft until after you are gone. Your plans are always a working document that will be consulted over and over again, so there is no excuse to not start. Immediately following this worksheet, you'll see a completed example, so you can see how some questions or blanks should be filled in. Tips are included to help you decide how to answer. Of course, your answers will be different and personalized—and that's the whole point.

How to Talk to Me After I'm Gone Worksheet
Information about me:

My statement of faith:

Designated medium for séances after death:

How will you know it is me if I contact you after I'm gone?

The intensity and type of interaction I offer after I'm gone:

Why my spirit will not be used negatively after death:

My preferred method to talk after I'm gone:

My hopes for frequency of interaction after death:

My preferred waiting period for contact after death:

In life, I was a passionate expert about the following topics, and I invite you to ask me about them:

The following offerings will please my spirit:

The following places are sacred to me, and will aid you if you contact me in such spaces:

Invocation chant:

My advance directive, will, and other important documents about my wishes are located here:

Alexandra's Worksheet (Example)
Information about me:
Alexandra Nicole Chauran, born Nicole Alexandra Pawlucki to Patricia Jeanette and Roy Nick Pawlucki. Mother to Eris Nikita Chauran and Orion Samuel Chauran. Wife to Derek Bryan Chauran, married on Samhain, 2005.

My statement of faith:
I am a Queen, High Priestess, and Elder of British Traditional Wicca. As a Wiccan, I believe strongly in spirit communication after death, and I invite people to ask my spirit to execute magical spells and to participate in sacred rituals. After I die, I would like a wake as my memorial instead of a funeral, and I would prefer cremation to speed my transformation to spirit. As an interfaith chaplain, in life I valued the diversity of faith traditions, so I invite anyone of any religion or lack thereof to talk to me after I am gone. For those who care for me and hope that I am well, don't fear.

I believe that after death I pass into the Summerland for rest in the arms of the Goddess. You need not bother to ask my spirit if I am happy or if I have reached the end of all suffering, because I believe I will continue to learn and to be presented joys as well as challenges and do not desire to be eternally untroubled. Rest assured that I am okay because all is as it should be. I believe I will choose to be reincarnated on this living planet again, because it is the best of all possible worlds. I am certain I will meet my loved ones again in my next life, remember them on some level, and love them again.

Designated medium for séances after death:

Since I would like to encourage anyone and everyone to contact me after my death, I do not designate anyone as a medium for séances after my death. There is no single person who holds a monopoly on contacting me.

How will you know it is me if I contact you after I'm gone:

Since I invite people to contact me themselves personally, I don't anticipate that the living will have much trouble with fraudulent mediums after I am gone. However, if you wish to find out whether I am speaking with you, ask for a sign and then listen for the bark of a dog or the croak of a frog. Even if the sound is distant, I hope that it will be a confirmation for you.

The intensity and type of interaction I offer after I'm gone:

I welcome chats about anything with my spirit. In life, most subjects were not taboo for me, so just having a conversation over a cup of tea is fine with me. As a magical practitioner, I support the use of spirits in magic. My spirit can carry out the actions of a spell or aid in the development of a magical exercise. My spirit can offer powerful protection for a person, place, or object. As a religious Wiccan, in life I invited spirits to attend and witness rituals, and I would be honored to visit your rituals in spirit.

Why my spirit will not be used negatively after death:
It is known that my spirit will retain control over its own actions and will not be commanded to do anything. If anyone attempts to so much as make a request that unduly harms or infringes upon the free will of another, the damage that was intended will not occur. In fact, the intended effect will come back to the perpetrator who made the rude request. Do not attempt negative use of my spirit, or else you'll find the tables will be turned and it will be you who are burned.

My preferred method to talk after I'm gone:
As a fortune teller, I've used many methods of spirit communication, and I hope my children and descendants will as well. If you are already comfortable using a method of spirit communication, you may continue its use with my spirit. For beginners and strangers, my preferred method of spirit communication will be the use of a spirit board. To make a sufficient spirit board, you will need paper, a pen, and a glass. Write upon the paper each of the letters of the alphabet, the numbers zero through nine, and the answers "yes" and "no." Overturn the cup on the piece

of paper and allow it to slide freely to indicate one of the characters on the page. When a message comes through from my spirit, flip the piece of paper over and write down the message.

My hopes for frequency of interaction after death:

No amount of contact is too frequent, as I believe that my spirit will not be bound by time in the same way as the living. However, I will not require that my loved ones talk to me daily, as I am inviting many people to talk to my spirit anyway. The best times to talk to my spirit will be on the holidays of Samhain, the last day of October and first day of November, and Beltane, the last day of April and the first day of May. Other excellent times to amplify my spirit's message are each full moon of the month. However, those with a desire to talk to my spirit need not wait for some special time. I can be reached by simply speaking aloud, even when performing daily chores. No time is too insignificant.

My preferred waiting period for contact after death:

I believe that the ideal period of waiting after my death for attempting communication is three days. Give time for proper arrangements to be made for my cremation to help release my spirit, and for my loved ones to deal with the mundane consequences of my transition. If more time is needed for grieving, take it with my blessing.

In life, I was a passionate expert about the following topics, and I invite you to ask me about them:

In life, I was considered an expert in the topics of fortune telling, witchcraft, and writing, so I hope to be especially helpful for people undertaking such tasks. In fact, I offer for people to attempt to channel books through my spirit after I am gone. In life I felt passionate about helping animals, children, and the mentally ill, so I hope to be a protective and healing influence for those groups as a spirit by request.

The following offerings will please my spirit:

I don't want the presence or absence of offerings to be limiting when deciding to talk to my spirit so if you have nothing on hand, that is okay. If you don't want to summon my spirit empty handed, a simple glass of water as an offering will do. My most favorite beverage in life was a simple hot cup of tea, so if you have hot water present, so much the better. The following incenses were preferred by me and will please my spirit: Frankincense, jasmine, patchouli, sandalwood, and rose petals plucked and dried. Blended all together, such incenses will provide a powerful aid for my spirit, but even one that is available will be helpful.

The following places are sacred to me, and will aid you if you contact me in such spaces:

Believing that doorways symbolically represent the liminal space between the worlds, I leave my instructions that those who wish to summon my spirit do so in a doorway facing out of the building, room, or structure. Even in an ordinary house, take yourself to any room or to the front door and stand looking outward. Lift both hands to rest them on the door frame and you may intone the following invocation chant.

Invocation Chant:

> Alexandra, word doctor, witch;
> close my eyes and count to three,
> conjure spirit where I sit.
> That magic and a future see—
> Blessed be.

My advance directive, will, and other important documents about my wishes are located here:

I have given copies of my important documents to my husband and to our lawyer. I encourage copies of my personal spirit communication instructions to be shared among those who wish to contact me.

From Worksheet to Step-by-Step Instructions

Even with a completed worksheet, the idea of spirit communication may seem overwhelming to a novice. That's why it is vital to introduce your spirit communication wishes before you're gone, and it is a great idea to experiment with talking to spirits with loved ones. Chapter 2 is all about how to begin communicating with spirits. You'll be able to grab your friends, but more importantly your loved ones, and have fun getting the hang of basic skills before they are a desperate necessity. We already discussed the nuts and bolts of spirit communication, so what follows is a cheat sheet on how to use a completed spirit communication worksheet.

Cheat sheet for how to contact a spirit using a completed worksheet:

Step 1) Gather your supplies: Has the person requested a specific offering such as food or a beverage that needs to be prepared? Do you need to purchase incense or flowers? Make sure that you have procured any appropriate offerings. Acquire any recommended divination tools and any pertinent instructions on how to use them.

Step 2) Wait for the right time: Has enough time passed after the death to proceed? Do you feel in sufficient emotional control that spirit communication won't negatively affect your grief process? Check to see whether a time of year or time of month is specified, and heed any instructions to limit your communication to times of important need, if indicated.

Step 3) Prepare the space: If the instructions suggest a specific place, go there. Chapter 2 includes tips and techniques for making any place a sacred and safe space. Display the offerings appropriately in the space.

Step 4) Invoke: Intone the invocation, if given, to invite the spirit into the space.

Step 5) Talk and thank: Use the suggested spirit communication technique. Thank the spirit to allow it to leave the space, and close down or clean up any special preparations you've done to the space.

Thus, you can see that even the most complicated fin- ial wishes can be laid out into simple steps. You can take the cheat sheet with you when you perform spirit com- munication yourself, or write in on a card to slip into your final plans along with a note about the location of your more detailed instructions. Review chapter 2 to become comfortable with spirit communication in more detail, es- pecially the example at the end of chapter 2 that shows you what it will look like when you put it all together. With a little practice, some of these steps will turn into second nature for you and your loved ones, and you'll more quickly and easily get to talk with people after they are gone.

Things to Consider

1. Make a list of all the people who know your material and spiritual plans for after death. For example, who knows what sorts of spiritual services you want performed after your death?

Who knows whether you prefer burial and cremation or details about your estate? Make another list of people in your life to whom you need to communicate these important things.

2. How do you best express yourself about deep topics? For example: Speaking aloud, writing, or even singing a song. Prepare a way to share your message.

3. Is spirituality a private topic or a public one for you? What are some of the advantages and disadvantages of taking your beliefs public and of keeping them private?

4. What positive feelings might you experience if you receive the ideal help and support from your loved ones about your spiritual beliefs? What would your life look like if everyone important to you was open to trying spirit communication?

5. Name some resources you can turn to while creating end-of-life plans. For example, someone who has experienced the death of a loved one or a lawyer who can prepare documents.

CHAPTER FIVE

Helping Others and Living Your Faith Out Loud

Can you imagine knocking on doors and trying to share the joys of spirit communication with people? You'd probably be even less well received than the average proselytizer. But when you do start spirit communication, you will want to share it as gospel, because the confirmation brings untold joys. Besides, without others close to you practicing, you'll have nobody who wants to talk to your spirit after you're gone. That brings a little bit of pressure with your joy. You're motivated to have people respond positively and actively to your interest. I have to hold myself back from asking strangers, "Have you heard the good news that life is eternal? You don't have to believe me. Try it, and you'll prove spirit communication is real within your lifetime."

Spirit Communication with Someone Who Will Die Before You

Chances are that you know somebody who is likely to pass on before you do, but you feel like that doesn't let you (or them) off the hook for talking about spirit communication. Perhaps your grandparents or your parents are people you'd want to contact after they have crossed over into the next world, but you want to get permission first. Wanting that permission before attempting to contact his or her spirit is admirable. After all, you've learned that there are a lot of particulars about which people may hold strong opinions.

First, remember that it's not the end of the world if you don't get a living person's permission before you contact his or her spirit after death. It is a tough job to give yourself under the best of circumstances. If a person is dealing with end-of-life issues, you should especially avoid such conversations unless you know the person would take it well. Don't make somebody else's dying moments all about you. Furthermore, after death some people might change their minds. My dad was pretty sure there was no life after death—boy, was he surprised! Give the spirit a chance to make up its mind when using the techniques in this book. It's always better to gently welcome rather than command to appear.

If, however, the death of your elder loved one is not imminent, the best approach is on several levels. For example, throw a spirit communication party and invite your loved one, give him or her a copy of this book, or just have a heart-to-heart talk. Don't try all of these at once, of course; the point of all these various attempts is to gently broach the subject with its many facets so that at least one way will be accessible to your loved one. This method also prevents you from stalling until some final moment. This isn't a proposal, like that of marriage; it should be an ongoing conversation.

Starting the dialogue

To paint a picture that illustrates this sort of exciting conversation with an older loved one, let's imagine that you tell them that you would like to talk to them about something important. You set aside some time and a quiet place to talk about it, so by now your loved one knows this is pretty serious for you and is prepared to listen carefully. Start by explaining that you want to talk about your faith and beliefs, and reassure him or her that you're not looking to convert anybody; you only want this person to be more familiar with your views.

Start by explaining that you believe in life after death and in spirit communication. Give time for your loved one to confirm or add on beliefs of his or her own. Be ready with references, but don't bombard your loved one with definitions and instructions right away. Instead, focus on opening the doorway of communication and practice active listening. Even if the other person disagrees with you, make eye contact, listen quietly and paraphrase what he or she says to make sure that you understand it correctly.

Example dialogue prompts:

- "It makes me feel comforted when I think about how I believe in ..."

- "So, you are saying that you believe..."

If things are going well, you can open up and say that you hope to communicate with your loved one's spirit after death, and see how it goes over. Even though you may be desperately seeking approval and support, keep the focus on how your beliefs help you and what your loved one can do to help you. The following are some things that you might say.

Example requests for permission:

- "I feel excited and comforted when I believe that I can contact you no matter what happens in our lives or deaths. Will you help me by granting your permission for me to speak aloud to you after you're not physically on this earth anymore?"

- "I worry that someday time and space will separate us. You can help me by supporting my beliefs. Can I count on you to let me try to talk with you even after you lay the troubles of this world aside?"

Hopefully, the answer will be a resounding yes. If you get anything less than that, don't apply pressure. Remember that the answers you are hoping for are a consolation for yourself rather than helpful to your loved one. If you've gotten this far, you've already opened up a line of communication about a very important topic, so consider yourself successful.

If, however, things go sideways because your loved one is coming from a faith tradition (or lack thereof) that doesn't approve of spirit communication, keep your chin up. Let your loved one explain his or her point of view, even if it involves condemning or venting. Again, this is just the point at which you are beginning the conversation, so even a confrontational start is a start. Practice active listening again, and wait until your loved one is finished sharing all that needs to be shared. Thank your loved one for caring, even if it feels uncomfortable. Show by your actions and your demeanor that your beliefs in spirit communication give you peace and make you a better person.

Making a plan—empowerment and resources

No matter how your conversations go, cheerfully continue with your multi-pronged approach to getting those around you on board with spirit communication. Even if you don't know where to start, you know that you'll want at least one or more persons ready to hear you after you are gone. Even the most unlikely of suspects might turn out to be incredibly enthusiastic about the idea. Don't be offended if somebody seems to be focusing on the differences between your beliefs rather than the similarities, as such explorations are just another way to find common ground.

A spirit communication party

I have had so much fun throwing spirit communication parties, and they've actually been a mainstay of entertainment for small dinner parties of adults since the mid 1900s. From séances to spirit board parties, they usually start out slow and timid and end with raucous laughter and spooky moments that reinforce our deepest spiritual beliefs. Here is the complete guide to a party that everyone is guaranteed to remember.

First, choose one method of spirit communication so as to not overwhelm your guests. I've had a lot of luck with spirit board parties because people vaguely know what to expect but it's still interesting. Choose a weekend night where people can enjoy some time in the spooky dark with your spirit board or other spirit communication method. Plan to invite anyone you can. You'll be surprised at who will want to show up. Some friends of mine have even invited friends from out of town or dates to my spirit board parties, knowing that it will be an unusual and memorable good time.

Invite your guests ahead of time and inform them completely of the activities to take place. You don't want to surprise your guests when they show up, as such an unusual activity makes many people feel uncomfortable. You may wish to give the party a theme, such as Halloween spookiness, or New Year's Eve reflections on the past. You might even serve themed food such as cookies shaped like ghosts. I like to buy wine with labels that use images or names that recall ghosts, skeletons, or other spooky things. Set up a few candles or go all out with decorations, and you're good to go. You can follow the séance procedures to have a great time.

Make sure to solicit feedback from your guests on the spot or by sending a thank-you note to all those who attended. You'll want to address matters right away if anyone felt uncomfortable during the party. Chances are, however, you'll find that people loved the party and have stories to share about dreams or other connections made with spirits afterward. Make a note of who had a very good time and plan another party to follow. If you make it a regular event, such as twice a year, you may start a little micro-culture that exists after you're gone. And perhaps you'll be the one attending those parties as a spirit in the future!

Finding local resources

Find even more friends who are into spirit communication in your local community and band together. If you have a local metaphysical bookstore, it would be a great way to ask about related events. If you're energetic like me, you may want to even become the point of contact for interested people. I've reserved a room at a library and advertised little discussion groups and classes in which we learn together from a book like this one. Check online for local groups and use the Internet as a resource for posting your own. It may seem like a strange thing to have in common with people, but I've found that spiritual discussion groups are a way to make friends for a lifetime. They often have other things in common with me as well and can be open minded about differences.

Starting a book club

Sometimes deep subjects are easier to approach with reading and discussion. Picture a group of friends meeting weekly or monthly to snack and chat about mind-blowing spirit communication books. Start a book club and read inspiring stories about talking with people after they have died. Check out the bibliography at the end of this book for suggestions. The "Things to Consider" questions at the end of each chapter can serve as book club discussion questions, too. Typically, a book club will read a chapter each week or month, or a book a month, depending on the speed the members prefer. Groups will get together for a potluck and chat about what they noticed during each reading, and thoughts they've had. A book club is a great way to make friends, and perhaps build the number of people who will want to talk with you after you're gone.

Try visiting a local book store or a library to reserve a space for your book club. They may be happy to not only give you a private space to discuss these interesting matters, but also provide a means of promotion for your group so your message can reach a wider audience. These days, you can even set up a book club online and discuss things at a distance if you're worried that you won't find any people interested in spirit communication near you. You might be surprised, however. Many people have an interest in the eternal.

Preparing for Your Own Death Joyfully and Unafraid

Preparing for death should be a part of life embraced as pragmatically as car insurance and umbrellas. Some parts of the preparation may not be very fun, but they can be made easier. The trick to standing up to a culture that fears death is to avoid losing perspective. Instead of placing death far from your mind where it can surprise, puzzle, and intimidate you, build it into your life so it doesn't dominate your thoughts or worries. These efforts can quell the little reptilian stirrings in the back of your mind that were designed to cause you to flee from death in less evolved times.

I organized this book in a way that prepared you with principles, so let's go over these instructions from the point of view of practice:

Integrate the celebration of ancestors into your everyday life. Make some practical arrangements right away, such as procuring furniture and decorations to create an ancestor altar. Set a pretty offering plate out every night when you set the table for dinner. You might want to put framed pictures of ancestors in with your holiday decorations boxes or dining sets to remember to sing songs and say prayers on their behalf throughout the seasons.

The best way to get through the hard stuff is with a to-do list. Set aside some time to work through any of the material preparations that are yet to be made. Make time to write or revise your spiritual plans. Make copies and distribute them to the necessary people and places. Plan a reward for yourself when you are done with the tough stuff. Next, you'll just need to get yourself to do some of the ongoing maintenance of your thoughts and of your spirit communication learning.

For me, it helps a lot if I put things in my daily planner. For example, at 8:00 am every morning I record any dreams I had when my alarm went off. I also enter in a repeating appointment to practice divination and meditate. I put the more sporadic things I need to do on my calendar as well. For example, I set up séance parties in advance. You can make a note on your own calendar to have séance parties during the best times of year to contact spirits, the end of April and the end of October.

I also make a point to set some dates to go through the boring paperwork, like my spirit communication plans and other end-of-life documents, to make sure they're still up to date with my wishes. To me, dates like my birthday and New Year's Day help me remember to check up on those things. You might want to choose other times, such as Daylight Saving Time. By linking your important upkeep to specific holidays or dates, you'll soon build it into your routine and memory from your calendar. As an added bonus, you'll connect yourself to the seasons by creating new traditions. Doing so will help you stay tuned to life changes and enjoy the time you have on this earth.

Getting Closer to the
Other Side—Talking to Deity

If you believe in the divine (or have the desire), promoting a connection to the source of power and creation can help you feel better about death and life. If you feel so inclined, reach out to form a connection with your chosen deity or deities through prayer, meditation, and worship. You can choose poetic prayers, or you can just talk out loud as if you were speaking with a friend. Prayer can leave one feeling empowered by having a loving source of divinity that has dominion over the worlds of the living and the dead. In some Christian faith traditions, God is a line of communication with spirits that you can use any time, like a divine voicemail where you can leave a message with your deceased loved ones. It renders unnecessary the use of any other props and techniques.

Ever wonder why hospitals that aren't run by a religious organization still have a spiritual care department and often a prayer room or chapel? In my time as a chaplain, I learned something interesting. Those who felt content with their relationship with divinity were those who experienced the most healing, and therefore an extended life. It wasn't the atheists who had problems. In fact, if they were content with their belief system, they were fine. But those who felt conflicted about their relationship with their higher power/s were the ones who had the most trouble healing and living life. As chaplains, it was our job to help them work through that feeling of conflict to a feeling of peace.

For people with a spiritual drive, connecting with divinity also brings great joy to life. People searching for material things in life won't find satisfaction no matter how much money, love, companionship, or comfort is acquired. Such people would do well to immediately fulfill their need for spirituality; it brings the kind of joy that's independent of external events.

Personally, my connection with my gods has gotten me through tough times of illness and of my life going off track, and has helped make the good times in my life seem more purposeful and bright. Seeking physical fitness or the perfect family or the perfect job isn't nearly as fulfilling to me personally as seeking the divine. Connecting with my gods is like forging a relationship with loved ones that will never be broken.

What does a connection with divinity feel like? The experience is different for everyone. I experience my gods in many ways; I can meditate and speak to them in the same way I speak to spirits during spirit communication. During ritual worship with my spiritual community, I see them in the faces of my family and friends. I can even do the work of the divine myself and be a part of something greater than myself. It's definitely okay if your experiences are not the same! Sometimes working with the divine can be merely comforting, reverent, or invoke a sense of coming home. As you get older, your relationship with your spirituality can change, and when you die and become a spirit, your relationship with divinity can change even more still.

Past Lives

Belief in past lives is a special part of many peoples' faiths. If you happen to believe in past lives, exploring this part of your faith is one way to grow in certainty about your own life persisting after the death of your present body. You don't have to remember a past life to believe that they exist. In fact, I don't spend a lot of time dwelling on my own past existences, and that's okay. I have work to do in this life, after all.

Learning lessons

One way to explore past lives is to figure out what lessons you may need to learn during this lifetime. For some people, that means exploring past lives to see what lessons have been learned in the past and what is still left to be discovered. In my work as a fortune teller, many clients come to me asking what or who they were in past lives and what those past lives might have to do with the present. Some come with memories of past lives experienced in dreams or senses of déjà vu when visiting certain places.

One reading involves placing three cards from a past life representing the body, mind, and spirit inhabited at that time. Next to these, three cards are placed corresponding to those same realms but in the present. A seventh card between them represents a lesson carried over to this life, yet to be learned. Sometimes, court cards can come up during such a tarot reading, in one case confirming past life memories for a client of mine who believe that he had once lived as a king in a past life. Other times, other memories will be confirmed in more symbolic ways, such as another client of mine who saw the Two of Cups and remembered a past life in which she struggled to connect with a lover.

You don't have to know advanced divination techniques to explore past lives, however. You can invite memories of past lives into your dreams through the same techniques used in chapter 2 to invite spirits. You can also simply allow your faith in past lives to inform the way that you live your life now by asking yourself what the important themes in your life seem to be. If patterns keep repeating themselves in your life, ask yourself what resources you need to stop any negative cycles so you will not carry them forth into your next life.

Meeting and remembering other people from past lives

This weekend, I had the pleasure of serving as an ordained clergy member officiating at the wedding of two friends of mine. These two friends were joining in marriage after years of being in a relationship; however, they knew early on that they were going to be married. They believed that they had known and loved each other in a past life, and that they would know and love each other in future lives to come. In fact, when I asked them whether they were planning to have children, they laughed and both said "not in this lifetime!" They both felt they had passed the age of childrearing this time around, but each was confident that they would reunite in a future life and perhaps raise a family at that time.

Reincarnation is a very important part of my Wiccan belief system, not just because we learn lessons each lifetime but also because it gives us another chance to reunite with our loved ones besides spirit communication. Even in our group worship settings, we believe that we seek each other out each lifetime to perhaps even circle together in the same covens. I am constantly on alert to notice people who appear in my dreams or with whom I seem to have an instant connection in life, curious as to whether I was an important part of their past lives.

For example, on the night of my initiation into a coven, I met a woman I had never met before in this life. In my practice of Wicca, members may remain secretive about their membership, so it can be a surprise to find out exactly which people you might be worshipping with when you first start. When I saw her, I was surprised and delighted because I had dreamed about her before. My instant connection with a person who was essentially a stranger was, to me, consistent with my beliefs that perhaps we had worshipped together before not just in my dreams but in a past existence.

If you also want to discover people who you have known in a past life, this is another good reason to work with your dreams and to take note of people your dreams may be urging you to meet. Pay attention to your intuition when you meet people with whom you have an instantaneous connection. Don't be afraid to share your beliefs, and to ask others whether they share your feelings. You might not only validate your own faith, but the faith of another kindred spirit.

Lead by Example: Spread the Word about Acknowledging Spirits

You can be part of the movement that accepts spirit communication and try to change the cultural perception of death. The more you develop and show your joy for life and spirit communication, the more others are likely to accept and share your beliefs. I've started a weekly spiritual discussion group in my home that quickly attracted a hodgepodge of earnest seekers of spiritual wisdom, confused people who felt rejected by their spiritual communities, and people who were bored on Sunday evenings.

Over the course of our time together, we've bonded, we've shared our stories both joyful and sad, and we've grown stronger in our faiths. At one point, our group was joined by a couple of Mormon missionaries who just happened to knock on the door. They didn't particularly approve of my means of spirit communication, but they agreed that the dead could help them come to know things that they could not otherwise come to know.

At one point, a friend of mine was sharing her feelings of being lost and then finding herself, and one of the Mormon missionaries quietly said, "This is a good place." Turning to me, he added, "This is a wonderful thing that you're doing." Even though our faith traditions were quite different, we could all recognize the growth and faith coming to the members of our little group. Here are a few specific lessons I learned that I would like to pass along to you.

Being unapologetic about death

When you refer to death, use the word "death," a tip I learned in my time as a chaplain. Using the word was actually more culturally sensitive; families wouldn't be confused when informed of the status of their loved one and wonder, "He passed away? Passed away where?" There was a story shared of a person who knew very little English who was told that his mother had expired. He simply thought it meant that his mother had exhaled and stopped breathing, and wanted to know when she would be "inspired" again.

The terms and euphemisms we have for death are used to put distance between ourselves and the topic. The idea that somebody has "passed on" or "crossed over" feels more comfortable than the idea of someone dying. However, when you begin to explore death, you will find that those concepts are one and the same, and don't have to be sugarcoated with language.

When the terms "death" and "dying" come up in conversation, use the words freely and be open about your own practices. When friends of mine lose loved ones, I always offer to help the family in any practical ways, but I also offer my prayers. A friend's grandmother died, and I asked if she thought her grandmother was the type who would want me to talk to her. Even in those dark days of grief, my friend managed a chuckle. She said her grandma wasn't the type and politely declined my offer. A few months later, however, I invited that same friend to a séance near Halloween, and she contacted her grandmother herself. I'm glad I made the offer and was open about my beliefs at the time of her grandmother's death; otherwise, I probably wouldn't have thought to invite her to the séance later and she might have missed out on a very joyful and life-affirming reunion with her loved one.

Volunteering and gaining perspective

Volunteering as a chaplain permanently changed my life and perspective on death. I was able to see all sorts of deaths, from ones filled with frantic attempts at rescue that brought tears to eyes of medical staff to peaceful deaths with harps playing in the background. Every day, I was able to see a person's last communications with their family members. Hands were held and important words of closure and comfort were shared. Most amazingly of all, I was able to be there as a spiritual caregiver at the moment of death. I was able to see the eyes of a person as they saw death or God or something unknown come for them. I experienced the presence of newly released spirits, and was able to talk with family members who could feel or even see their loved one's spirit.

After spending the day tending to people in their last moment of transition into death, going home left me happy and appreciative of my own life. It's hard to get mad at spilling a cup of tea after getting some severe perspective. I also found myself fearing death much less. Instead of death being a mysterious thing that appears in horrifying or tragic news stories, volunteering pulled back the curtain, revealing that it was just another stage of life.

Being a volunteer hospital chaplain is pretty intense, and it is not for everyone. However, you can volunteer in ways that form positive associations with life and death cycles. If you're brave, you can volunteer at a hospital, hospice, or nursing home, even if you're just doing paperwork. If working directly with people isn't your thing, there are plenty of graveyards that could use maintenance, maybe you could keep weeds at bay and replacing wilted flowers with fresh ones. A photographer friend of mine volunteers for genealogy websites by taking photographs of gravestones, and he is also a fan of photographic orbs, the representation of spirits on photographs that are thought to appear around some graves.

Even my young children volunteer in a way that acknowledges end-of-life issues, by coming with me to cheer up the residents of a nursing home. We meet and talk with a specific resident in particular who would otherwise never get visitors and who is confined to his room. My kids have learned to love him, and he took the time to teach me the sign language alphabet. I know that one day he will die, and I will have to explain to my children as much of the nature of death as they are able to understand when that time comes. I believe, however, that such an experience will leave them richer for it.

Inviting others to remember you by leaving a legacy

Everybody wants to leave something good behind after death. Chances are you already do this, through your interactions with children or other people who will survive you, and the ripples of goodness you send out into the world with every smile you share. Famous psychologist Erik Erikson wrote that near the end of one's life is a phase during which one tries to wrap up unfinished business, check items off the bucket list, and leave a positive mark on the world. You don't have to be nearing death to get started on that wonderful phase of life. In fact, getting a jump on leaving a legacy will help you feel more positive and relaxed about your life as you are living it.

Leaving a legacy looks different for different people. For me, it involves writing books like this one. For others it might mean going back to school to become a teacher, blogging, building houses for the homeless, teaching family members a secret family cookie recipe, donating money to an animal shelter, or giving enough blood that the center puts up a little brass plaque with their name engraved on it. You could even leave a legacy by making your spirit communication instructions public and causing conversation (and possibly controversy) in the process.

You can take a small step toward leaving a legacy today, even if it is just doing a little research about your goal. When you die, you and your spirit can be remembered for something tangible here on earth. In a way, you will be taking big steps towards becoming a more honored ancestor, as seen in many cultures; your reach will extend forward into the hearts of the future.

Setting up a workshop

After reading this book, you probably won't feel like an expert in spirit communication, but compared to the rest of your community, you probably are. Community outreach is one way you can solidify your own beliefs, counteracting our culture's fear of death and bringing spirit communication into the mainstream. Besides, teaching something is the best way to learn. With this book, you're fully equipped to teach a workshop to help people continue to communicate with their loved ones after they have died.

Start by finding some space to hold your workshop. Metaphysical bookstores, New Age wellness centers, and psychic or New Age fairs and festivals may have space available and a process for teaching workshops. If those resources aren't available, you can look for meeting space at your local library, community center, or even just a coffee shop or pub. Advertise locally with fliers, online, and by telling your friends. Here is a sample curriculum for such a workshop.

Sample Workshop Curriculum
Length: 1 hour

Materials: Copies of the *How to Talk to Me After I'm Gone* worksheet, pencils (optional: strips of paper with "Things to Consider" discussion questions from the end of the chapters for longer workshops; divination tools for people to examine and try).

Objectives

Skill: Students will be able to create their own instructions for spirit communication.

Value: Students will value spirit communication as one way to cope with death.

Introduction: Introduce yourself and share a personal story about spirit communication.

Activity: Lead the students through completing the worksheet by explaining each entry as they work. Let them work independently for about thirty minutes, walking around the room to help individuals who get stuck or have questions.

Evaluation: Go around the room and ask students to share their feelings about, and hopes for, spirit communication. Optionally, you can break into small groups and give each group a discussion question from one of the chapters of this book to extend the workshop. If you have divination tools, each small group can be given one to examine and try.

Sharing the subjects and attitudes in this book
with your community and the world at large

Teaching a workshop and starting discussion groups and regular séances will probably make you feel pretty confident about your beliefs. I know that I tend to evangelize my faith in life after death as much as the average missionary talks about his or her religion. I'm not yet knocking on doors and asking people if they've heard the good news about spirit communication, but if I had the time, it certainly would not be outside the realm of possibility!

I do, however, find plenty of more appropriate moments to bring up my beliefs; during times of loss, when the seasons change, near Halloween when everyone is thinking about ghosts, and wherever there is an opportunity to learn and teach about great spiritual questions. I hope that you too will keep alert for these great opportunities. You may find that you build a pretty healthy attendance at your séances this way. My husband often jokes that I should start my own church with the regulars who show up at my house.

An Invitation

Before we wrap up this chapter, I would like to leave you with a final note of encouragement and a demonstration of how much faith and excitement I find in this process. I'd like to invite you to contact me after I'm dead. Make sure I'm dead first, please, because I can't say that I'll come running when you call while I'm still too busy loving this amazing thing we call life. As a testimony to my lack of fear about people contacting me after I've died, I'd like for you to try it, should you outlive me. It is my sincere hope that people continue to communicate with me after my death. I know that other people have similar wishes. This knowledge should spur you to reach out to those who are already deceased and to prepare for your own future life after death.

Things to Consider

1. Think of a life event that gave you some perspective and helped you stop worrying about the little things. It may have been anything from a medical emergency to a joyful milestone. How can you rekindle those feelings in your life without reenacting that particular transformative event?

2. How do you currently feel about sharing your faith? What circumstances or inner thoughts make it harder for you to speak openly about your beliefs?

3. What are some spiritual skills or pieces of knowledge you have that other people may not already know, even if they are just tidbits you've learned recently? How can you reach out and offer that knowledge back to the community to leave a legacy?

4. What are your everyday, ordinary skills? How can you volunteer them in a spiritual capacity within your community?

5. Who are the deceased people (celebrities or otherwise) with whom you would like to get in touch? Do you know other people who might also be interested in such a thing? What are some local resources for holding a public discussion group or even a séance?

Conclusion

Imagine the spirit of a woman who has just died. One moment she was driving along, hurrying to get home from work, and then nothing. Unbeknownst to her, she had been thrown into a coma due to a violent car accident. She passed the next several weeks in a white haze of suspended life until her family made the decision to withdraw life support. Paradoxically, she regained awareness as her spirit slid out of her body, sloughing her mortal form like a snake's skin.

As she rolled in a newly fluid existence, gaining her bearings, she could still remember her name—Sarah. She looked down and recognized the faces of her grieving family, wanting to hug them. The worries of life seemed so close and yet so far. She knew there were some basic, practical matters she should be worried about: How was

her family going to pay for the funeral? Was her will updated? Where did she hide that thing, anyway? However,
all those details seemed to hum in the background of her
consciousness without affecting her deeply. As a spirit,
Sarah rose above the droning buzz of humanity, feeling
content that things would all work out for the best.

Sarah glanced down at her body, which now looked
like just an empty vessel, almost plastic. She followed her
family out of the hospital room and drifted home with
them without hesitation. There was nothing more that tied
her to anything she didn't wish. Over the next few days,
Sarah was desperate to communicate with her loved ones,
but retained that sense of calm detachment from the world
of the living that allowed her to give them space to grieve
in peace. She knew that in time, they would be ready.

It was Sarah's sister who reached out to her first. The
attention of Sarah's spirit was snatched away from mar-
veling on the beauty of eternity in an instant, when Sarah
heard her name whispered by her sister. In an instant,
Sarah was in the room of her sleeping sister. Lily, her
little sister, had just whispered Sarah's name in prayer before sleep, hoping to meet her in her dreams. The horizon
melted away as Sarah dove into Lily's dreamscape.

At once, it was as if they had never been separated.
Lily's subconscious allowed her to forget for a moment
that Sarah was dead. Sarah's spirit existence allowed her
to feel that strange calm. In a dream field, they held hands,

laughing and weeping over nothing, just happy to be together. "You can still talk to me," Sarah urged, wanting Lily to never feel alone. Sarah pulled out a dream version of her spirit communication instructions and pressed it into Lily's hands like a talisman, willing her to remember where the real instructions were placed, not relying on her own hazy memory of the living world.

This book was meant to be written. I had a dream about living my spirit life. When I saw this book in the dream, I immediately told my publisher. I received a positive response on 12/12/12 and signed the contract in about a month, which is lightning speed in the publishing industry, let me tell you. My editor observed that this book must be good therapy for me, and it was. At the same time, it has been the hardest to write because I care about the subject matter so much and truly believe I am gifting an important responsibility to the world.

I'll gladly admit my own imperfections and agree that it is hard to think about our mortality. As many people drag their feet when drafting a will for their families or buying life insurance, I wrote this book slowly and haltingly. Writing these words is admitting that I'll die, so the act seems final. While writing, a niece was born. I added her name to the dedication, thinking about how I couldn't wait to get to know her as she grew and help her in this lifetime and the next. Even though this will not be my last book, it is my final book spiritually—my legacy. It is the one that will allow me to keep speaking (and even writing) through people like you when I die and transition to my existence as a spirit guide.

Maybe you'll have to set goals and add little deadlines to your calendar to prepare for spirit communication in this life and after you die, like I've done. I truly hope that you will and that you'll share the good news that we can all keep on "keeping on" after death.

When I set out to write on life after death and spirit communication, it was to address this essential question: "What good is my belief in spirit communication if nobody talks to me after I've died?" Now, I'd like to ask you a follow-up question: What good can you do with spirit communication after you die? This moment is the beginning of your legacy and the beginning of the good you can create in the world now and forever. You have been given the gift of everlasting influence…What are you going to do with it?

Appendix: Resources

Billion Graves—At BillionGraves.com you can upload photos of your local cemetery's headstones to help others find the graves of their ancestors.

Dead Social—At DeadSoci.al you can secretly create messages to be released on your social networks after you die.

Find a Grave—FindaGrave.com is another opportunity to volunteer your photography for people who are searching for proof of the grave sites of their ancestors.

Get Your Sh*t Together—There are free resources for paperwork such as wills and advance directives as well as other basic planning at GetYourShitTogether.org

Ifidie.net—Create video messages through a Facebook application. The videos are only released after you die.

Let's Have Dinner and Talk About Death—A start-to-finish resource for having a conversation about death and your plans over dinner. http://deathoverdinner.org/

My Gift of Grace—A game designed to stimulate conversation about death and end-of-life plans. http://mygiftofgrace.com/

Bibliography

Al-Chokhachy, Elissa. *Miraculous Moments: True Stories Affirming that Life Goes On.* Woodbury, MN: Llewellyn Publications, 2010.

Anthony, Mark. *Never Letting Go: Heal Grief With Help from the Other Side.* Woodbury, MN: Llewellyn Publications, 2011.

Aurelius, Marcus, and George Long. *Thoughts of Marcus Aurelius Antonius [Kindle Edition].* Seattle: Amazon Digital Services, Inc.

Brock, Ginny. *By Morning's Light: The True Story of a Mother's Reconnection with Her Son in the Hereafter.* Woodbury, MN: Llewellyn Publications, 2012.

Buckland, Raymond. *Buckland's Book of Spirit Communications.* Woodbury, MN: Llewellyn Publications, 2012.

———. *Solitary Séance: How You Can Talk With Spirits on Your Own.* Woodbury, MN: Llewellyn Publications, 2011.

———. *The Weiser Field Guide to Ghosts.* San Francisco: Red Wheel, 2009.

Danelek, J. Allan. *The Case for Ghosts: An Objective Look at the Paranormal.* Woodbury, MN: Llewellyn Publications, 2006.

Drake, Linda. *Reaching Through the Veil to Heal with Loved Ones in Spirit: Death, Grief & Communicating.* Woodbury, MN: Llewellyn Publications, 2007.

Eynden, Rose Vanden. *So You Want to Be a Medium? A Down-to-Earth Guide.* Woodbury, MN: Llewellyn Publications, 2008.

Konstantinos. *Summoning Spirits: The Art of Magical Evocation.* Woodbury, MN: Llewellyn Publications, 2012.

Lejuwaan, Jordan. "The Wim Hof Method Revealed: How to Consciously Control Your Immune System." *High Existence.* 29 March 2013. http://www.highexistence.com/the-wim-hof-method-revealed-how-to-consciously-control-your-immune-system/.

Mathews, Patrick. *Forever With You: Inspiring Messages of Healing & Wisdom from Your Loved Ones in the Afterlife.* Woodbury, MN: Llewellyn Publications, 2012.

———. *Never Say Goodbye: A Medium's Stories of Connecting with Your Loved Ones.* St. Paul, MN: Llewellyn Publications, 2003.

Owens, Elizabeth. *How to Communicate With Spirits.* St. Paul, MN: Llewellyn Publications, 2001.

Parkinson, Troy. *Bridge to the Afterlife: A Medium's Message of Hope & Healing.* Woodbury, MN: Llewellyn Publications, 2010.

Serith, Ceisiwr. *The Pagan Family: Handing the Old Ways Down.* St. Paul, MN: Llewellyn Worldwide, 1994.

GET MORE AT LLEWELLYN.COM

Visit us online to browse hundreds of our books and decks, plus sign up to receive our e-newsletters and exclusive online offers.

- **Free tarot readings • Spell-a-Day • Moon phases**
- **Recipes, spells, and tips • Blogs • Encyclopedia**
- **Author interviews, articles, and upcoming events**

GET SOCIAL WITH LLEWELLYN

Find us on

Facebook
www.Facebook.com/LlewellynBooks

Follow us on

www.Twitter.com/Llewellynbooks

GET BOOKS AT LLEWELLYN

LLEWELLYN ORDERING INFORMATION